BARNES & NOBLE BASICS™

home renovation

by Ela Schwartz

**BARNES
& NOBLE
BOOKS**

NEW YORK

For information, contact:
Barnes & Noble, Inc.
122 Fifth Avenue
New York, NY 10011
212-633-4000

Other titles in the **Barnes & Noble Basics**™ series:
Barnes & Noble Basics *Using Your PC*
Barnes & Noble Basics *Wine*
Barnes & Noble Basics *In the Kitchen*
Barnes & Noble Basics *Getting in Shape*
Barnes & Noble Basics *Saving Money*
Barnes & Noble Basics *Getting a Job*
Barnes & Noble Basics *Using the Internet*
Barnes & Noble Basics *Retiring*
Barnes & Noble Basics *Using Your Digital Camera*
Barnes & Noble Basics *Getting Married*
Barnes & Noble Basics *Grilling*
Barnes & Noble Basics *Giving a Presentation*
Barnes & Noble Basics *Buying a House*
Barnes & Noble Basics *Volunteering*
Barnes & Noble Basics *Getting a Grant*
Barnes & Noble Basics *Getting into College*
Barnes & Noble Basics *Golf*
Barnes & Noble Basics *Your Job Interview*
Barnes & Noble Basics *Résumés and Cover Letters*
Barnes & Noble Basics *Starting a Business*
Barnes & Noble Basics *Personal Budgeting*

introduction

"We really need to maximize the space in our house," sighed my friend Nora. "With Ben working from home and two little boys running around, we have no room to breathe. I want to renovate, but I am terrified at the thought. Where do we begin? How do we choose someone to do the job? How much is it really going to cost?"

Stop and take a deep breath. **Barnes & Noble Basics** *Home Renovation* is here to help take the stress out of your renovation project. This handy room-by-room guide will help you avoid common renovation pitfalls. Ever wonder why your contractor must be licensed, bonded, and insured? See page 34 on choosing a qualified contractor. Learn which renovation projects increase the value of your home the most and how much you can expect to pay for them (see page 12). Discover why smart wiring now can save you time and trouble later on (see pages 110–111). And much more.

Whether you're adding a second floor or simply updating the bathrooms, *Home Renovation* has all the expert advice you need. So turn the page and start making your dream home a reality today.

Barb Chintz
Editorial Director, the **Barnes & Noble Basics**™ series

table of contents

Chapter 1

Getting ready to renovate

preparing to renovate

From dream to reality

Great, you are ready to renovate! It's a big decision that says a lot about you. It says that you are ready and willing to change your physical surroundings to better reflect your life now. Perhaps you have a small house, and now that the children are teenagers, you need more room. Or maybe it's time to convert an unused bedroom into your dream library or home office, or put in that spa bath you have always wanted.

When it comes to renovation, most people have a hard time honing their wishful thinking into concrete improvements. One way to flesh out your ideas is to create a renovation portfolio. Buy a loose-leaf binder, accordion file, or pocket folders. Create files for things you want to change; for example, you could name a file Kitchen or you could get really specific and create one called Lighting Fixtures. Next, go through magazines and cut out pictures of rooms or features that appeal to you, such as particular flooring types or appliances. Go to home improvement centers and start collecting product brochures, paint chips, fabric swatches—anything that inspires you. File these dream clips in your renovation portfolio.

THE SAME STYLE WE SAW IN SHOWROOM

FROM MARVIN WINDOWS & DOORS BROCHURE

OASIS

TETON

SAVANNAH

DUNE

Next, start prioritizing. The first rule is to renovate for the life you really lead. Why remodel a seldom-used dining room or guest room if you really only use it a couple of times a year? Think about turning that empty room into space you can use. If you're an exercise buff, for example, then think about creating a home gym. Love to read? Turn it into a library. If your children like to play music, make it into a music room. In other words, think about what you really enjoy doing, then concentrate on how your home can be remodeled to best accommodate your wants and needs.

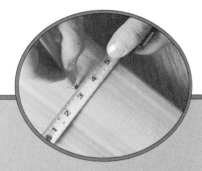

THINKING IT THROUGH

Your portfolio of clips is burgeoning. Great. From time to time, sift through them and think about what you want to do. Start with one room you want to change. Draw a rough layout of the area of the room. Next, consider these five key elements:

1. Function What is the purpose of the room? Keep a list of what goes on in the room during the day and night. Could you repurpose the room? Turn a playroom into a home office? Turn a basement into a state-of-the-art laundry and sewing room?

2. Traffic flow How could you improve traffic flow? Remove a wall? Change the furniture around?

3. Light Does the room get enough light? Where could you add windows? Are there enough outlets for additional lighting fixtures?

4. Storage Is there space to put things away so the room isn't cluttered? Would a built-in unit or window seat help? Would a new closet or mudroom keep the coats and sporting equipment from cluttering up the family room?

5. Temperature Is the room too hot or cold? Too damp or dry? Does it have proper insulation? Would a ceiling fan do the trick? Is there enough electrical power for an air conditioner? Can you replace older windows with more energy-efficient models? Sketch the positions of any new items on your layout. If you're ambitious, you can use a tape measure and graph paper to get a more accurate rendering.

the stress of renovating

Think before you leap

Yes, remodeling is a major investment of money and time. You'll need to develop plans, hire professionals, and choose and buy supplies, not to mention put up with the inconvenience of construction and possibly demolition. That all spells stress—lots of it.

Renovation can also take a steep emotional toll. If you're renovating with a partner or spouse, be prepared for lengthy negotiations on everything from which contractor to hire to what color tile grout to use. For all these reasons, renovation is not to be undertaken lightly. Also, it's probably not the best idea to embark on a renovation when you are in the throes of major life changes, such as having a baby, getting married, getting divorced, finishing a degree, changing jobs, or dealing with health problems.

You should also think about your house and your neighborhood. You don't want to renovate a home that you may be leaving in a few years. In fact, the rule of thumb is don't renovate unless you are fairly certain you will be staying in your home for at least five more years.

Smart reasons to renovate

1. You're happy with your house but want to improve its looks and/or function, or add extra space, and your changes aren't extensive.
2. You are content with the size of your lot.
3. You have friends in the area.
4. Your community offers amenities you enjoy, such as shopping, parks, recreation, and safe streets, that you would have difficulty finding elsewhere.
5. You and your kids are happy with the schools in your school district.
6. You have a very easy commute.
7. Property values in your neighborhood are rising.

Ask the Experts

I want to renovate my home, but I'm worried about the toll it might take on my young family. Would moving be better than renovating?

While remodeling can take an emotional toll, moving can as well, especially if you're moving to a new community and not just down the road. Think about it. You'll be leaving your old life behind and will need to make new social contacts and adjust to a new community. And moving is particularly wrenching for children, who become very attached to their homes, schools, and friends. The good news is that renovating is typically less expensive than moving. According to the American Homeowners Foundation (**www.ahf.org**), if you sell your home and move to a new one, you'll pay about 8 percent of the value of your home in closing costs (6 percent) and broker's commission (2 percent), and possibly another 2 percent on moving costs. If your home is worth $200,000, that's as much as $20,000. Think of the changes you can make on your existing home for that 10 percent!

I've always wanted to renovate my home, but a real estate agent just told me that my town is suffering an economic downturn. Should I still renovate?

Ideally, you don't want to renovate a house in a community where the property values are stagnant or declining. The aim is to recover your renovation costs eventually, and in a down market, that can be very hard. If you are certain you will be staying in your house for at least five more years, then make only the changes that you really can't live without, because you don't want to have the most improved house on the block in a down market. A good rule to follow: A renovation should not raise the value of your house to more than 10 to 15 percent above the median sale price of other houses in your neighborhood.

resale potential

Improvements that add value

A renovation can be one of the smartest investment decisions you'll ever make. Not only will it enhance your enjoyment of your home, it can also pay for itself should you decide to sell your house. But not every renovating project is created equal. A kitchen or bathroom remodel, a family room addition, a master bedroom/bath remodel, and a deck are all relatively safe improvements to make. Not so a state-of-the-art media room or a pool.

Here's a news flash. In an upmarket, your renovation costs will most certainly be recouped should you sell your home. But since not all renovation improvements pay out equally, how do you know which renovations give the most bang for your buck? Thankfully, analysts in the renovation industry know the answer. Here is a list of renovation projects that typically yield the greatest returns on investment:

Project	Cost	Amount Recouped	Percentage
Deck addition	$6,304	$6,661	104%
Siding replacement	$7,329	$7,247	98%
Midrange bathroom addition	$15,519	$15,418	95%
Attic bedroom	$32,863	$30,500	93%
Upscale bathroom remodel	$23,544	$23,457	93%
Midrange bathroom remodel	$10,088	$9,890	89%
Upscale window replacement	$15,577	$16,168	87%
Midrange window replacement	$9,568	$8,673	85%
Upscale bathroom addition	$38,349	$32,272	84%
Family room addition	$53,983	$43,931	81%
Upscale kitchen remodel	$68,962	$56,711	80%
Basement remodel	$43,865	$34,801	79%
Midrange kitchen remodel	$43,804	$33,101	79%
Upscale master suite	$133,993	$103,279	77%
Midrange master suite	$70,760	$54,376	76%

Source: *Remodeling* magazine, 2003 Cost vs. Value Report

Ask the Experts

Will an upscale renovation always recoup most of its value?

No. It all depends on how upscale your neighborhood is. Watch out for over-the-top renovations. Granite surfaces and commercial-grade appliances are fine for luxury homes, but are less likely to pay off in moderate-income neighborhoods. A local real estate agent can be an excellent source of information about what potential homebuyers in your community are looking for.

I want to install bright pink tiles in my bathroom and put in a shell-shaped lavatory. Will this come back to haunt me if I have to sell my home?

As much as we love to turn our homes into personal statements, let your furniture, window treatments, and accessories express your personality, and keep permanent fixtures—such as tile, sinks, and flooring—simple and neutral-colored. Don't forget there is always the outside chance that you may tire of those pink tiles one day!

FIRST PERSON DISASTER STORY

His-and-hers decision styles

When my husband and I decided to renovate, we hired an architect to help us. Things were going great until we saw the architect's drawings. I thought they looked fine and reflected all the things we had discussed, but my husband took one look and changed his mind about the master bath and the screened-in porch. More drawings were done and my husband had more changes, and on and on it went. The architect's bills started to pile up, so I told my husband that we had to either put off the renovation until he knew what he wanted or decide once and for all. He sheepishly agreed. He went back to the magazine clips he liked and realized that the drawings were fine.

Erica S., Bedford, New York

more space, please

Extensions, dormers, and reconfigurations

Renovation is often about space: not having enough of it or not having it where you need it. One way to get that extra space is by extending a room beyond your house's footprint (the perimeter and inside area of the foundation). An addition can entail expanding a room or building one or more new rooms on the ground floor, upper floor, or both.

While the results are often dramatic, an addition can be one of the more expensive renovations, not only in dollars but in increases to your insurance and property taxes (see page 22). You'll also need to check your community's zoning regulations (local land use rules

that determine what structural changes you can make, including how high buildings can be and how much they can cover your lot). Expanding upward may require laying an extra foundation and/or doing structural work, so you'll need an architect or structural engineer to determine if your house can handle the extra load.

Instead of adding square footage, you can convert unused space into livable rooms by finishing a basement, attic, garage, or porch. You can also reconfigure your existing living space by, for example, removing a wall to open up a kitchen or expanding a bathroom by stealing space from an adjacent bedroom or closet.

Remember that even relatively small changes can make a big difference. Adding windows can make rooms feel more spacious. An upstairs single dormer (a window projecting through a sloping roof) opens up a room visually, not to mention giving you more head room or storage space. Just keep in mind that adding and closing up windows is more expensive than replacing them.

Ask the Experts

Is there a way to extend a house that won't be as expensive and labor-intensive as building an addition?

You can add what's called a bump-out, which is a small addition of approximately four to six feet. Your existing roof and foundation can most likely handle the extra load. You will, of course, be punching out a wall and will have to make sure you're not removing a load-bearing wall (see below) or one that contains electrical or plumbing lines that would need to be relocated. As with any structural change, check with your engineer or architect. Although a bump-out won't give you as much extra room as a larger extension, it's enough to accommodate a bay window, window seat, bathtub, or extra kitchen counter space.

MORE THAN JUST A WALL

Moving a wall can dramatically change the layout of your home. But make sure you know what kind of wall you're dealing with. A nonbearing wall separates rooms but provides no support, so it's usually not a problem to remove these. If you remove a load-bearing wall (a wall that helps support the house), you can find yourself with sagging walls and ceiling—or worse—unless you put in a header. This is a horizontal beam that carries weight over openings such as windows and passageways.

That's not to say that you have to call it quits on removing a load-bearing wall. Consult an architect or engineer, who may be able to draw plans for redistributing the wall's load. You may be able to remove part of the wall and install columns, which will provide the necessary support while opening up the space visually. Or you can install a header. This is a horizontal beam that carries weight over openings such as windows or passageways.

evaluate your home's condition

Identify critical repairs and upgrades before renovating

Before undertaking a renovation project, check the condition of your home. Why? Because you don't want to spend money putting a whirlpool tub in the master bath, for example, only to find that your ancient hot-water heater doesn't hold enough hot water to fill it.

There are two things to consider: 1) the health, well-being, and age of your furnace, central air conditioner, and hot-water heater, and 2) the state of your house's structure. Look for cracks in the foundation, which mean the house is settling (shifting or sinking in the earth). Make sure gutters aren't leaking, and that downspouts (vertical pipes) are directing water away from the foundation. Check the condition of your roof and look for evidence of water damage in the attic. While you're at it, check ceilings and walls for discoloration caused by a leaking pipe. Also look for sags in walls or floors that signify structural damage.

If you don't feel up to doing the job yourself, hire a qualified inspector to complete an inspector's report: a detailed checklist of the house's structural condition and major systems. The American Society of Home Inspectors (**www.ashi.org**) maintains a searchable database of certified members who have conducted at least 250 individual inspections. The National Academy of Building Inspection Engineers also offers a member directory at **www.nabie.org**.

Depending on the problem, you'll want to repair it before or during a renovation. There's no better time than when a wall is open to replace insulation, plumbing, and electrical wiring, and conversely, there's nothing worse than tearing down a freshly painted wall to do a repair job. Also consider upgrading systems while you are renovating. Think about it: The walls are being ripped out or opened up anyway, so now is the time to upgrade your wiring or install better plumbing or state-of-the-art cable.

A GUIDE TO YOUR HOME'S SYSTEMS

Heating, ventilation, and air conditioning (**HVAC**) This includes your furnace or boiler, ducts (these disperse the heat or air-conditioned air), fans, water heaters, and air conditioning and ventilation systems. If you're expanding living space, make sure your HVAC can cover the extra load. Note: If your boiler is 10 or more years old, consider trading up to a more energy-efficient unit.

Insulation Your HVAC works hand in hand with insulation and weatherization. If walls feel cold, you'll want to check the quality of your insulation. Insulation is measured in terms of R-values—the higher the value, the better the insulation. Check for drafts, especially around windows, and eliminate them by using caulk and weather stripping or by replacing windows (see page 104).

Electrical Check to see that you have enough grounded outlets (outlets that accept a third prong) and ground fault interrupter (GFI) devices in bathrooms and kitchens. An electrician can decide whether you'll need additional dedicated circuits, or separate lines, with separate breakers to handle a power-hungry appliance like a hot-water heater or refrigerator. Think about your wiring needs both now and for the future. You may want to wire now for a phone, a cable TV, an intercom, or a security system (see page 110).

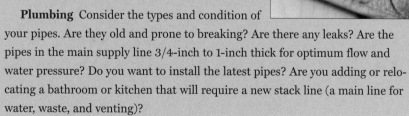

Plumbing Consider the types and condition of your pipes. Are they old and prone to breaking? Are there any leaks? Are the pipes in the main supply line 3/4-inch to 1-inch thick for optimum flow and water pressure? Do you want to install the latest pipes? Are you adding or relocating a bathroom or kitchen that will require a new stack line (a main line for water, waste, and venting)?

architects and designers

Balancing looks, cost, and maintenance

Some folks have a real knack for renovation projects, but if you're like most people, you'll probably want the help of professionals.

If your renovation doesn't involve new construction or structural changes, an interior designer can help you choose materials and make design decisions, such as recommending windows to brighten up a dismal dining room.

If you will be making structural changes, hiring an architect is the best route. Even if a designer or contractor draws up your plans, the final working plans—or blueprints—will have to bear the stamp of a certified architect or structural engineer before your town will issue a building permit (see page 32).

Working with an architect has many benefits. Part artist, part engineer, part psychologist, architects are skilled at visualizing how your renovation will fit with the rest of your house and at translating renovation ideas and dreams into reality.

Architects also create detailed plans, which reduce the likelihood of mistakes, confusion, or change orders (written requests to use different items or materials or to modify the renovation from what was specified in your original contract). Change orders can add to your expenses considerably if they're issued during the construction phase of a project.

In most renovations, the architect's role ends when the plans are completed. But you can also hire an architect to manage the entire project for you, including getting bids, hiring the contractor, and overseeing the work. If you're not very assertive, you may appreciate being able to delegate the responsibility of informing your contractor that the walk-in closet he's building is a foot shorter than what was specified in the plans. However, keep in mind that a brilliant conceptual designer may not be the best organizer and vice versa, so it's important to decide which skills are a priority and find an architect who fits the bill.

Ask the Experts

How do architects and interior designers charge for their services?

An architect may charge a fixed fee for the total price for the job, a percentage of the total construction costs (typically 8 to 10 percent), or a rate of approximately $100 per hour. Interior designers usually charge on a cost-plus basis (cost of items plus a 15 to 20 percent markup), or $50 to $100 per hour.

What do I do if I'm getting cold feet at just the thought of the extra money involved in hiring an architect?

Relax. Hiring an architect is not an all-or-nothing deal. If you're unsure, arrange for a consultation. An hour-long meeting will cost around $100, depending on your area. Call a few architects and ask their rates. Some architects will waive the fee if you decide to hire them. Even if you don't, you could walk away with ideas and solutions that will make the visit worthwhile.

A ROUND-UP OF RENOVATION IDEAS TO CONSIDER

Open-plan living Rather than a separate kitchen, living room, and dining room, these three rooms merge into one open "great room."

Kitchen as hub of the home Kitchens are getting bigger and more elaborate, with areas for meal preparation, socializing, and even computer desks and sofas.

Spa baths Bathrooms have evolved from utilitarian necessities into personal spas, sporting such amenities as whirlpool tubs, dual sinks, and even televisions and phones.

Master bedroom retreats The combined master bedroom/bath addresses the need for personal yet shared space. Bedrooms are roomier, often with a sitting area and walk-in closet.

Outdoor rooms Porches, decks, and patios have become veritable outdoor living rooms, featuring grills, lighting, and furniture worthy of indoor use.

Better storage Take control of your stuff by utilizing built-ins, shelving, and storage systems that keep belongings out of the way but not out of reach.

budget basics

Getting a handle on costs

Renovating can be costly, so try to get a grip on expenses before you start. First things first: how much can you afford? Consider your monthly expenses and settle on a monthly remodeling payment that you can handle comfortably.

Renovation costs fall largely into three categories: 1) materials, 2) amount of materials used, and 3) labor.

Measure each area you plan to remodel, then use these numbers to price materials at home improvement or decor stores, or on manufacturers' Web sites. As you add things up, you may have to make some tough decisions to stay in your budget. Try simplifying your project or choosing less expensive materials.

Labor is another big budget item. If your job is fairly small, call craftspeople or contractors and ask for an **estimate** (approximate total cost). For a bigger project, get a handle on labor costs during the design process by asking your architect or designer about this. Don't confuse an estimate with a **bid**, or the final cost agreed on in your contract (see pages 38–39). And be aware that final bids often come in higher than even the most careful estimates.

Once you get an estimate, create a contingency budget by putting aside an extra 10 to 20 percent for glitches. Ripped-out walls often reveal leaks, termite damage, or other surprises. It's also a good idea to budget for take-out food and a few nights in a motel while your renovation is underway.

Two kitchen renovation budgets

To get a sense of how kitchen remodeling costs can vary, compare the two budgets on page 21. The first is for a basic kitchen, using stock cabinets and economy appliances. The second is for a deluxe kitchen with an island, hardwood cabinets, and high-end appliances. Note that these budgets don't include costs for hiring an architect or designer, or for more extensive structural, electrical, or plumbing work (often necessary in older homes).

ITEM	BASIC KITCHEN		DELUXE KITCHEN	
	Description	Materials	Description	Materials
Plywood (underlayment)	For 6'6" by 14' room	73.73	For 11'6" by 14'6" room	147.46
Wall and base cabinets	4 wall and 2 base cabinets, economy	1,101.60	9 wall and 9 base cabinets, hardwood	6,804.00
Flooring	Vinyl composition tile	78.00	Maple strip with 2 coats polyurethane	669.00
Countertop and backsplash	Formica	78.03	Granite	2,664.00
Valance board	Over sink	37.20	Over sink and bookshelf	74.40
Molding	Crown (stock pine)	51.07	Cornice (stock pine)	37.15
Paint	Primer, one coat, trim	32.46	Primer, one coat, trim	20.52
Stove	30" wide, one oven	304.80	Cooktop with griddle	642.00
Range hood	30" wide, two-speed	42.60	42" wide, custom stainless-steel	906.00
Refrigerator	19 cubic feet	600.00	Side-by-side, water/ice dispenser	3,330.00
Dishwasher	Seven-cycle	304.80	Built-in, seven-cycle	338.40
Sink with faucets	Self-rimming, single bowl	296.40	Self-rimming, double bowl	534.00
Rough-in, supply, waste, and vent for sink, dishwasher	One system	102.00	Two systems	204.00
Contractor's fee, including materials	$ 6,108.00		Wall oven	1,026.00
			Microwave	492.00
			Island cabinet with maple top	576.00
			Shelving	35.04
			Desktop	111.60
			Six recessed ceiling lights, 100-watt	399.60
			Undercabinet fluorescent strip light	247.20
			Contractor's fee, including materials	$ 32,324.00

Figures reprinted with permission from RS Means' *Interior Home Improvement Guide 2002*.

hidden renovation costs

Check all the angles before you start

In addition to unexpected budget busters like leaking pipes that need to be replaced or a crumbling foundation, you should prepare yourself for other indirect costs that result from making changes to your home.

For example, some improvements will cause your property taxes to increase. Adding extra living space, such as an upstairs or downstairs addition, can often lead to a tax boost. Aside from these biggies, municipalities differ on which improvements qualify for tax increases; some will raise your taxes if you add a fireplace, others if you put in an additional full bath, but not a half bath. Your best bet is to check with your town and find out if your project is likely to cause a tax increase.

Your renovation could also raise your homeowner's insurance premium, because all major improvements and additions increase the insurance coverage you'll need. Call your insurance company, explain your renovation project, and find out how the amount you're spending will be reflected in your premiums. You could find that certain changes, such as adding a security system or smoke alarms, may actually decrease your insurance payments.

Other hidden costs may include extra insulation or having to upgrade wiring if codes have changed since your house was built.

Finally, take a look at the added maintenance costs that may result from your renovation. This hidden cost of renovation often comes as a surprise to homeowners. If you're adding extra space or finishing an attic or basement, you'll not only have to install heating, ventilation lines, and electrical wiring, but also pay for heating, cooling, and lighting the new room.

Ask the Experts

Looking at all these hidden costs, I'm not sure I can afford a major renovation right now. What less expensive things can I do to improve my home?

If your main complaint about your home is looks, a little redecorating may do the trick. A new piece of furniture, window treatments, carpeting, or area rugs can make a huge difference in your home's appearance, and they don't require hiring someone to tear down a wall or put in a new floor, not to mention buying expensive building materials. With a little more effort and a little extra cash, you can sponge-paint walls, install decorative moldings yourself, or tile a kitchen backsplash.

SOFTWARE TO HELP YOU MANAGE RENOVATION COSTS

There are plenty of software programs that can help you put together and manage your renovation budget. Punch Software's Punch! Professional Home Design Suite-Platinum includes both design capabilities to help you visualize your project and a Home Estimator program that compiles your design information into a printable spreadsheet that is compatible with Microsoft Excel. Budget and accounting software programs, such as Intuit's Quicken or QuickBooks Pro, let you create budgets, track your transactions, and keep track of how well you're staying within your budget. Some even enable you to download your banking, credit card, and brokerage  transactions so that you don't have to type them in. Be aware that software manufacturers sometimes offer different versions of their programs, including everything from bare-bones varieties for $30 to small-business applications for $500 and up, so be sure to check the specifications before you purchase one.

financing options

Loans to see you through

If you have the cash to finance your home renovation, great. But the vast majority of people finance home renovations with some sort of loan. Most banks offer some very accessible loans that use your house as collateral (a guarantee to the bank that covers the loan should you forfeit on it).

If you need less than $10,000, you can apply for a home equity loan. Home equity is the amount your home is worth minus the amount you owe on your mortgage. The interest on this type of loan

is tax deductible and interest rates are usually low. When you apply for a home equity loan, the lender will look at your credit rating, credit history, current debt, cash on hand, collateral, and employment history to determine your interest rate and monthly payment.

You can also apply for a lump sum or installment loan, in which you withdraw a set amount and repay it in monthly increments. The interest rate is usually fixed, which benefits you if rates are low. Or you can choose a line of credit loan, in which you and the lender decide on a maximum amount and you make withdrawals as needed. This type of loan usually carries an adjustable rate, so leave room in your budget for higher monthly payments if the prime interest rate rises.

If you took out a mortgage when interest rates were higher, you might want to refinance, or take out a new mortgage at a lower rate. This can lower your monthly mortgage payment, freeing up some cash to use toward your renovation. You can also take out a bigger mortgage to pay off your existing mortgage and "cash out" the difference to pay for your improvements.

Confused? There are plenty of Web sites that explain financial terms and answer common questions. A good place to start is **www.borrowsmart.org**, a consumer service provided by the BorrowSmart Public Education Foundation.

Ask the Experts

Can I pay for my renovation with a credit card?

Yes, but it's not a good idea. While paying with a credit card can save you the time of researching and applying for a loan and waiting for approval, you won't be able to deduct the interest. Moreover, the interest is much higher than with a home equity loan. You're better off using credit cards to pay for materials under $5,000. Just be extra sure you'll be able to make your monthly payments on time.

My banker said that my debt-to-income ratio was above his bank's accepted percentage. What does that mean and what can I do?

Your debt-to-income (DTI) ratio is your total monthly debt divided by your monthly income. Lenders use this ratio to determine if you can shoulder the extra debt of a renovation. If your DTI ratio is 50 percent and your bank's limit is 30 percent, you can try to find a lender who will accept a higher ratio. Or ask your banker if you can apply for a debt consolidation loan, in which you roll your current debts into a home improvement loan. Since the loan is tax deductible, this solution provides one easy payment for your debts and lowers your DTI percentage. The interest on the loan may also be lower than what you're currently paying.

Where to apply for a loan

You have a few options. You can try a local bank or savings and loan, though they may not necessarily get you the best rate. A mortgage broker will shop around to get the best rate, but the downside is that brokers tend to hit you with the most fees. Web sites like **www.eloan.com**, **www.lendingtree.com**, and **www.bankrate.com** are good sources for comparing lenders. You may even be able to fill out forms and apply for a loan online.

now what do I do?

Answers to common questions

Do I have to research zoning regulations and setbacks before starting a renovation project?

Will your renovation be visible from outside your house? New windows, additions, dormers, and even decks and patios are subject to zoning regulations. If you want to build any type of addition, look into setbacks, requirements that houses be a minimum distance from the street and property lines, and easements, rights of access that neighbors or utility companies may have on some portion of your property. If you live in a historic house or planned community, your home may be subject to a restrictive covenant, which can limit or forbid certain kinds of alterations, including changing the roof, building an addition or pool, or other exterior changes.

When I remodel, how much clean-up should I expect the contractor to take care of? And how can I cut down on the dust and mess?

Most contractors will handle removing debris and possibly sweeping the area. You could specify more detailed clean-up in your contract, but don't. Why? You'll pay extra, and cleaning isn't really what contractors are good at. A better plan is to hire a professional cleaning service, or take care of the cleaning yourself with a good vacuum and mop at the end of each working day. Then treat yourself to a professional cleaning when the project is done.

To cut down on dust and mess during the renovation, have your contractor put up dust shields, or plastic sheeting fastened with duct tape, across doorways or openings of the room(s) being remodeled. And in your contract, specify which rooms of the house the crew will have access to and whether they can smoke. If the dust is really out of control, rent a high-efficiency particulate air (HEPA) filter for the duration.

The renovation we want would price us out of our local market. What should we do if we love our neighborhood and our house and don't want to move?

Sometimes the decision to move vs. renovate may come down to a gut decision. A large-scale remodel that will bring you years of happiness in a house and community you love may be worth the risk of not recouping your financial investment down the road.

Does the government offer any home improvement loans?

If your home equity is limited, you may want to apply for a Title I loan from the Federal Housing Administration (FHA). The loan can be used for certain alterations, repairs, and site improvements, including those that make your home more energy-efficient or accessible to someone with disabilities. You borrow from a lender approved to make Title I loans, and the FHA insures the lender against possible loss. To be accepted, you must have a good credit history and be able to repay the loan in regular monthly installments. The maximum amount of the loan is $25,000, and the maximum loan term is 20 years. You may qualify for other federal loans if you plan to fix up a home in a blighted area or historic district.

How do I know if my fuel bills are high or low?

Look at your bills and compare them to those of your neighbors, or ask your fuel company the typical price of heating a house the size of yours. If your bills are noticeably higher, have an independent energy audit done to help pinpoint your problem areas.

Now where do I go?

BOOKS

Successful Homebuilding and Remodeling: Real Life Advice for Getting the House You Want Without the Roof (or Sky) Falling In
by Barbara Buchholz and Margaret Crane

This Old House Heating, Ventilation and Air Conditioning: A Guide to the Invisible Comforts of Your Home
by Richard Trethewey with Don Best

The Healthy Home Handbook
by John Warde

Better Homes and Gardens: New Remodeling Book: Your Complete Guide to Planning a Dream Project

Bob Vila's Complete Guide to Remodeling Your Home
by Bob Vila and Hugh Howard

WEB SITES

The American Homeowners Foundation
www.ahf.org

The National Association of the Remodeling Industry
www.nari.org

The Healthy House Institute
www.hhinst.com

Homestore.com
www.homestore.com/home-garden/homeim-provement/remodeling

American Society of Home Inspectors
www.ashi.org

Remodeling magazine
www.remodeling.hw.net

Chapter 2

Working with professionals

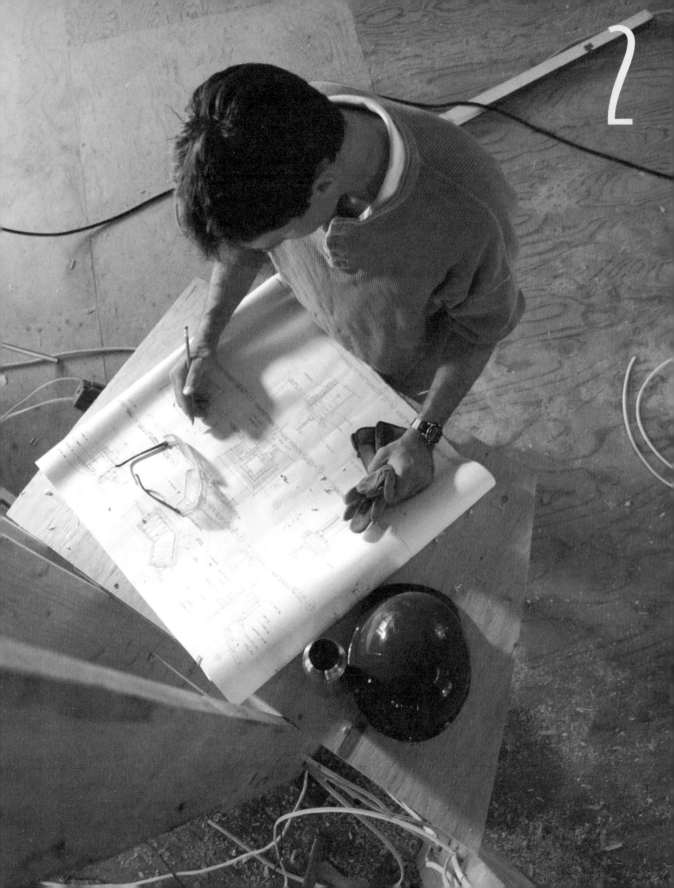

renovation professionals

Who they are
and what they do

Who will you hire to do your remodeling? Your team can include designers, builders, and numerous tradespeople. Who you'll want to bring on board depends on the scope of your project and the degree of specialization involved. Rest assured that there's someone out there to help, no matter what task is involved.

Architects are trained and certified to design buildings (see page 32). If your renovation involves changes to your home's systems (electrical, heating, plumbing) or structural changes, you'll need an architect or structural engineer to design or approve your plans.

If you're building an addition, it's a good idea to have a certified engineer check the suitability of the land and your house's structure and foundation.

A **contractor** or **builder/contractor** is the person who will oversee the construction of your remodeling. Contractors often started out as carpenters. Although it's possible your contractor will pick up a hammer, most spend their time coordinating the project, scheduling inspections, and overseeing subcontractors.

A design/build firm has a designer and contractor on staff who will handle your project's design and construction.

Subcontractors are the carpenters, plumbers, electricians, and other tradespeople that your contractor or designer will hire.

Specialty designers focus on different types of design. Interior designers design rooms and choose materials and furniture. A certified kitchen or bath designer specializes in the planning and layout of kitchens or bathrooms. A lighting designer is skilled in lighting a room to its best advantage. A landscape designer plans the arrangement of outdoor structures and plants.

There's another important member of your team: your building inspector. Hired by the town, he or she will approve plans and periodically inspect your renovation and determine if it meets the requirements of local building codes, local regulations that mandate construction methods and materials (see page 32).

Ask the Experts

How can I decide whether to use a design/build firm or a separate designer and contractor?

It's a matter of personal preference. Using a design/build firm provides you with a well-matched designer/contractor team in one interview. Instead of bidding on your project (see page 38–39), the design/build group will draw up plans and give an estimate. If you decide not to use them, you can pay for the drawings and find your own contractor. Design/build is a fairly new trend in residential construction, so there may not be as many of these firms as individual designers and contractors. The Design/Build Institute of America (**www.dbia.org**) has more information.

Our architect highly recommends a contractor she works with. Should we just go with him?

Great, you've found a contractor who works well with your architect. But don't sign him up just yet. You don't know if you'll get along with him, how high his bid will be, or how his other customers felt about him. Perform the necessary background checks (see page 35). Interview and get bids from other contractors for comparison. Don't feel pressured to use this person.

UNIVERSAL DESIGN

Make sure your architect or contractor knows about universal design. This is a design practice that accommodates all people, including those with disabilities, such as someone who uses a wheelchair or walker. Think about installing a ramp alongside stairs leading to one of your home's entrances—for example, the door coming in from the garage. If you are putting in new doors, reframe doorways to increase the clearance to at least 36 inches so that users of wheelchairs and walkers, as well as baby strollers, can pass through unencumbered. To prevent slips, use soft, nonskid surfaces on tub bottoms, shower floors, and stair treads and landings. Install grab bars in showers. For more ideas, contact the Center for Universal Design (**www.design.ncsu.edu/cud**).

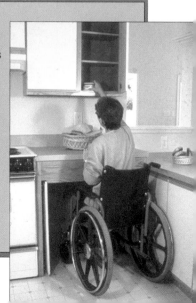

the design process

From plans to reality

Think of your plans as the road map and instructions that tell the contractor how to translate a two-dimensional design into a working room.

Once you've gone over your ideas with your architect or designer, he will draw up rough sketches of what your remodeled room will look like. Go over these sketches and let him know of any changes, which he'll incorporate into a new set of drawings. When you're happy with these drawings, they evolve into preliminary plans. These are more detailed drawings showing the placement of doors, windows, and electrical, plumbing, and heating lines and specifying materials. These, too, get critiqued and modified until you approve them.

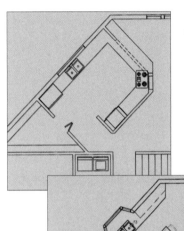

When you sign off on the preliminary plans, the designer creates the even more detailed final plans, which consist of the blueprints, or architectural plans, along with specifications, or spec sheets, which are detailed descriptions of materials to be used. These are the plans that your final price and contract will be based upon. They'll also be filed with your local building department.

What does the building department have to do with your renovation? Plenty. Changes to your home's structure and systems require getting a permit, or legal document issued by your town that gives you permission for doing the construction. Once the permit is approved, your town will schedule inspections, in which a town inspector visits your home and makes sure the work is up to code.

Your renovation project starts with a set of blueprints and plans.

Building codes are there to protect your health and safety, and sometimes the environment. Every municipality has building codes that specify materials and construction techniques. Although it's your architect or contractor's responsibility to be knowledgeable about codes, it's always a good idea to call or visit your local Building Department. Other organizations that can help: Building Officials and Code Administrators International (**www.bocai.org**) and the International Code Council (**iccsafe.org**).

Ask the Experts

Who applies for the permit?

This should definitely be handled by your designer or contractor, and specified as such in your contract. They've applied for permits before and know the process. The person who applies for the permit will also be responsible for having your renovation comply with building codes, meaning that if the construction doesn't meet code, you're the first person the inspector will turn to. That said, there's nothing wrong with stopping by the building department and running your plans by an official. They may be able to give you some helpful information and prove useful allies during your remodeling.

My contractor looked at the architect's designs and started pointing out possible changes that would save me money. Should I take his advice?

You certainly could. Experienced contractors often have good design ideas that can work well for you. To be sure, run his suggestions by your designer. If he seems put off by having a contractor suggest changes, you can always get a third opinion by consulting another designer.

My blueprints don't look anything like a real room! How can I tell what they're describing?

Good for you for admitting what every layperson is secretly thinking when looking at a blueprint. Blueprints are filled with unintelligible symbols and abbreviations denoting wall switches, water heaters, stairways, and just about anything else you could find in a room. Ask your architect or designer to explain them for you and decipher what the symbols mean or recommend a book that does. Understanding the final plans lessens the chance you'll have to make costly changes during construction.

evaluating contractors

A checklist of qualifications

You're about to embark on a quest: hiring the best contractor for your project. This quest is filled with phone calls, appointments, paperwork, and technical terminology. Yes, this part may not be as fun as designing a layout or shopping for fixtures. But you'll get through it, promise!

What is your image of a contractor? A supportive confidant who can create masterpieces out of mayhem? Or an ill-mannered lout who will wreak havoc and skip town with your money? Luckily, most contractors tend to fall into the first category. Your job now is to do plenty of research to find a trustworthy, competent contractor who will oversee your project from start to finish.

First, compile a list of names. Word of mouth is a good place to start. Ask friends, relatives, and coworkers who have renovated about their experiences with contractors. Your architect or interior designer, or a trusted plumber or electrician, may give you some names. Managers of lumberyards and other suppliers can refer you to contractors they do business with (and who pay their bills). Lenders, real estate agents, and even your town's Building Department are also good sources. Professional organizations like the National Association of the Remodeling Industry (**www.nari.org**) can give you a list of contractors in your area.

You can also check out newspaper ads and your telephone book. But a word of advice: Stay away from contractors who solicit business door to door or stuff flyers into mailboxes.

How many names do you need? Renovation experts recommend calling at least five to eight contractors, interviewing about five and asking three to submit final bids. Don't be dismayed if you call five and find only two you like. Just carry on! Gather more names or move on to the next ones on your list.

News flash

Licensing isn't everything. In fact, some states don't license contractors at all! For those that do, licensing can mean as much as passing an examination or as little as registering and paying a fee. Find out what your state's licensing requirements are. If there's no official licensing board for contractors, try the Department of Consumer Affairs or the Building Department.

CONTRACTOR BACKGROUND CHECKS

Now it's time to call around and ask contractors questions prior to setting up an in-person interview with those that make the cut. Make sure the contractors meet these criteria:

Licensed Ask the contractor if he's licensed and for a licensing number. Then check the number with your state's licensing board. Verify that the name and license number match and that the license is current.

Bonded Contractors pay a bonding company a premium to insure they'll complete the work to your satisfaction. If they don't deliver, you can collect some compensation. Note: This amount may not be sufficient for a large renovation, in which case you may want to purchase a completion bond from a bonding company, which will provide more extensive financial protection (see page 43).

Insured Make sure the contractor carries workers' compensation, as well as property damage and personal liability insurance. These protect you from litigation if anyone is injured on your job.

Clean complaint record Call your local Better Business Bureau or attorney general's office and run a complaint check.

Member in good standing of a professional organization Ask him for the name of the association, a phone number, and a Web site address; then verify his information with the organization. Two of the better known are the National Association of the Remodeling Industry (**www.nari.org**) and the National Association of Home Builders (**www.nahb.org**).

Years in business Try to find someone who has been in business at least five years.

interviewing

You've narrowed down your list of contractors. Now it's time to set up some in-person interviews.

Arrange to meet at your house. Ask each contractor to bring proof of license and insurance, a list of 5 to 10 references, and photos of his work. After your meeting, call the contractor's insurance company to make sure the policy has not lapsed. For your part, have photocopies of your plans on hand for the contractor to look over, and take plenty of notes during and after the interview.

You'll want to ask the following questions:

1. What type of projects do you specialize in? You want someone with experience with the kind of room remodel you're planning.

2. Will you be the one supervising my job, or will it be handled by someone else? If he'll be contracting your job to a supervisor, request to meet with the supervisor before hiring.

3. When would you be able to start work on my project? How many other projects will you be working on along with mine? The last thing you want is an overwhelmed contractor or one who doesn't show up at your job because of other commitments.

4. Will you be performing any of the work yourself? Construction is highly specialized. Stay away from contractors who tell you they can save you money by doing plumbing or electrical work themselves.

5. How do you prefer to get paid? The most common payment method is the fixed-price contract, in which you decide on the total cost of the job before work begins. You usually pay a percentage up front, make additional payments in one or more installments over the course of the job, and pay the balance, about 15 to 25 percent, upon completion.

Look at the contractor's ability to communicate effectively. Note if he becomes impatient or seems stymied by any of your questions. These are warning signals that you may not work well together.

CHECKING REFERENCES

Your interview is over. Whew! But wait, there are still some very important people you need to call—other homeowners like yourself who hired the contractor before.

Call at least five references. Ask them when the job was performed. Were they happy with the quality of the work? Did the contractor finish the job on schedule? Was he easy to get along with? Did he stay in touch throughout the project? Did he require a lot of supervision in order to get the work accomplished? Would they hire him again?

If their project was similar to yours, ask if you can visit and see the final product. Don't take it personally if the homeowner refuses. Not everyone is up to having strangers drop by for a house tour. Thank the person anyway, and move on to the next reference.

But wait. These references are people who were happy with the contractor. How do you know how many of his customers were dissatisfied? Easy. Every job your contractor performed that required a building permit is on record with your town's Building Department. Call or visit the department and ask for the names, addresses, and phone numbers of some additional homeowners who aren't on the official list. Pick the most recent jobs. Then call those people and ask the same questions.

You can also check out contractors with your local consumer agencies or the Better Business Bureau.

It's also a good idea to request business references. These are the suppliers the contractor buys materials from and the subcontractors he hires. Find out if the contractor paid them on time and if they ever had to place a mechanic's lien, a claim made against a homeowner's property, on any of his customers.

the bidding process

Cheapest is not always best

When you're done interviewing, look over your notes and narrow down your choices to the contractors whom you will ask to submit a **bid** (an outline of work required and a proposed fee) on your project. Choose at least three to five contractors. This will provide you with a good basis for comparison.

Contractors base their bids on how labor-intensive a project is. They also look at the cost of materials, including everything from lumber and heating ducts to appliances and tile. The bids should, at the very least, itemize the prices of subsystems such as masonry, framing, and HVAC, plus the cost of hiring various subcontractors.

Contractors vary in how minutely they'll itemize your bid. The more precise, the better. It shows the contractor really knows his stuff, and it will give you a clear picture of where your money is going.

You'll be looking at the total price, then comparing bids side by side to see where costs differ. Did anyone leave out any labor or materials costs the others included? Quote you prices for materials that weren't the ones you specified? Fail to list the appropriate subcontractors? If there's more than a 25 percent difference in the bid prices, ask the contractors if the plans were specific enough.

Note: In the contracting world, one person's bid is another person's estimate. In other words, some contractors will call this itemized price quote an "estimate," and the final price quoted in your contract the "bid." For others, the estimate is more of a "guesstimate," an educated guess on the price range of your project, this itemized quote is the "bid," and the last amount is the "final bid." Confused? Just make sure you and your contractors are on the same page when it comes to terminology.

Ask the Experts

What should I do if my first-choice contractor submits a bid that's too high?

Negotiate. Tell him that the bid is beyond what you feel comfortable spending. Many contractors will come down in price if it means getting the job. Ask if he has ideas on how you can cut costs. Ask why the bid came in so high. Maybe his experience has taught him to stick with experienced subcontractors who charge more. Or he just might have plenty of work and feel your job is only worth his while if he can command a higher fee. Weigh his answer and decide whether the higher price is worth it for you.

Should I just go for the contractor with the lowest bid?

A general rule is not to choose the lowest bid. The premise is that the contractor could be "lowballing" you, or submitting an unrealistically low figure in order to nab your job, then tell you after construction has started that you'll need to revise the contract because he underestimated and will need more money. A very low figure can also mean the contractor didn't complete an accurate bid. Or that he really needs the work. If you can't put your finger on why the bid came in lower, you're best off going with someone else.

contracts

Getting your agreement in writing

You've made the big decision and chosen a qualified, experienced contractor. Congratulations! All your effort has finally paid off. Now it's time to get your agreement in writing by signing a comprehensive contract.

A good contract details everything from materials to workmanship to schedules. It will spell out the brand and model number of a dishwasher and the R value of the insulation you want to use as well as the labor involved to install them. It will specify exactly where items are to be located and how the labor is to be performed. Instead of, "replace windows," it will read more like, "will remove current casement window on living room wall and replace with manufacturer model No. X casement window with double-paned glass and make sure window is operable."

Don't feel rushed into signing a contract. Take a few days to read it carefully, and make sure you understand and are happy with it. If your chosen contractor is a true professional, he'll be happy to answer your questions.

If you're unhappy with the contract he gives you or just want to get a better idea of what a remodeling contract looks like, you can purchase a sample from the American Institute of Architects (**www.aia.org**) or the American Homeowners Foundation (**www.ahf.org**).

You can also have a real estate attorney draw up the contract. A cheaper alternative is to ask one to look it over. Depending on the size of your renovation, this can be a very prudent move. Far better to pay a few hundred dollars now rather than a few thousand in legal fees down the road should anything go wrong.

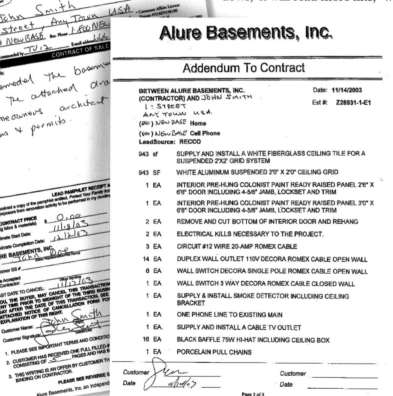

WHAT EVERY CONTRACT SHOULD INCLUDE

The date, your name and address, the contractor's name, address, license number, and phone and fax numbers, the location of the job site (your home), plus details on any other supervisors or project managers.

Specifications of materials and labor.

A schedule, including the start date, completion date, and dates when certain jobs will be finished, and a payment schedule noting the amounts and date of the down payment, final payment, and any other payments. Some homeowners include a late-completion penalty, in which a certain sum is deducted for each day the project goes past the agreed completion date. An alternative is to offer a financial incentive for work completed on schedule.

A work stoppage clause, which gives you the right to cancel the contract if work is deemed unsatisfactory or gets inexplicably delayed (see pages 42–43).

Details on how disputes will be handled, i.e. mediation or arbitration (see pages 44–45).

A provision specifying that work will comply with building codes and that the contractor will obtain all permits and schedule inspections (see pages 32–33).

A warranty for labor, and details on how change orders, or written requests for job changes, will be handled. Plus, a statement that the contractor will obtain lien waivers, which are written statements that absolve you from having to pay subcontractors and suppliers (see page 42).

Days and hours of work, cleanup procedures during job and on completion, and any other work habit issues you want to include.

A right of recision, which enables you to cancel the contract within three business days after signing it.

Copies of the contractor's personal-liability, property-damage, and worker's-compensation insurance policies and your blueprints and specifications.

other important documents

Change orders, lien waivers, and warranties

Don't worry, we're getting to the end of all the technical terms. Just a few more documents to go, and you'll be talking contractor lingo with the best of them.

Even though you've revised your plans umpteen times and signed a contract specifying exactly what your renovation will be, there's a chance you could change your mind about something. That's the purpose of a change order, which is a written request to alter items or work from what was specified in the contract.

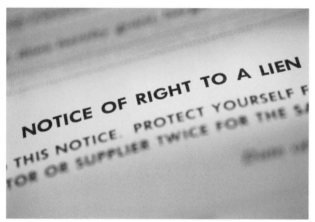

The change order should spell out the job, materials, cost, and time involved. These changes may require extra work and supplies, returning items, and possibly paying a restocking fee to put the items back into a store's inventory. It may even mean undoing work that's already been completed. Getting it in writing keeps everything legal and protects you and the contractor.

If your contractor fails to pay a supplier or subcontractor, they can file a mechanic's lien, which is a claim made against your property. Once construction has begun, don't pay your contractor until he provides you with a lien waiver, which is a document signed by each supplier or subcontractor who performed work stating that they have been paid and will not file a lien on your property.

Most contractors issue a warranty, a written guarantee covering defective construction work for a given period, usually a year. Make sure your contract contains a warranty clause stating as such.

In addition to the contractor's warranty, you will be receiving manufacturers' warranties on everything from the appliances to building components like flooring and windows. Find out exactly what the warranty covers and for how long.

Ask the Experts

How can I avoid making and paying for change orders?

Sometimes change orders can't be avoided. Your contractor may discover termites or asbestos that needs to be removed. Other times, you could issue a change order because you decide that the wallpaper that looked perfect in the showroom doesn't cut it on your living room wall. Or your contractor may suggest a change, perhaps adding a skylight to your master bedroom. Don't let change orders get out of hand—they can send your budget skyrocketing. Weigh the costs against your happiness. You don't want to spend years staring at that wallpaper or feel pangs of regret when you look at your skylightless ceiling. This is your dream project, after all.

What is a completion bond? Do I need one?

A completion bond is a type of insurance you purchase from a bonding company. The bond acts as a guarantee that the contractor will complete the work in accordance with the specifications of the bid. If he fails to do so, the bonding company will pay you for any monies lost on the project or additional expenses incurred. A bond will cost you around two to three percent of the total contract price. If your renovation is extensive, and expensive, a completion bond can provide additional protection. Your lender or real estate attorney can help you find a bonding company.

That final payment

As an extra precaution, don't issue the final payment to your contractor until 30 days after the completion of the job. This is the period of time allowed in most states for suppliers and subcontractors to file a lien against your home.

firing a contractor

Arbitration, litigation, and moving on

What if things aren't working out between you and your contractor? How do you proceed?

Firing a contractor isn't a simple matter. That's because contractors don't like completing work started by someone else. Even if you find one willing to take on the job, they probably won't offer a warranty on their labor.

So your first step is to try to talk things over and resolve the situation with Contractor #1. You never know, he may be as uncomfortable with the situation as you are. If talking one on one doesn't work, you can seek mediation, in which you and the contractor sit down with an impartial third party and discuss your differences. Both of you must agree to the mediation, and the decision is nonbinding, meaning you are under no obligation to abide by what the mediator suggests.

Most contractors and homeowners prefer arbitration to going to court because it's less costly. Your arbitrator sets a hearing date, and you present your case to an impartial third party, as in a court hearing. Find out if the decision will be binding or nonbinding to either party.

If arbitration doesn't resolve the dispute, firing your contractor may be the answer. Be sure to provide a work stoppage clause in your contract (see page 39). This provision gives you the right to fire the contractor if work isn't performed as specified in your contract.

If you're seeking compensation for damages, you can go to small claims court. "Small claims" means exactly that, so check the financial limits in your state. If your amount exceeds the limit, remember that you can sue separately for each offense—for instance, one time for having the roof replaced and another for damages the rain did to your hardwood floor.

Ask the Experts

Where can I find mediation and arbitration services?

Your community may offer mediation services for little or no charge. Other sources include the Better Business Bureau and the local bar association. You can find arbiters through the American Arbitration Association or your insurance provider. As with any legal matter, it's always a good idea to consult a lawyer.

How should I prepare for an arbitration or a court hearing?

Bring your blueprints. Take plenty of photos documenting the problem. Talk to your designer and have him appear with you or sign a statement attesting that the work was not done according to plan. Ask your friends or neighbors to witness on your behalf. Bring any invoices submitted by a repairperson who had to fix shoddy workmanship. Talk to subcontractors and suppliers and find out if they're having any bad experiences. You may not be the only one having problems.

FIRST PERSON DISASTER STORY

Look before you leap

I decided to hire a contractor friend of mine to remodel my upstairs. Because I trusted him, I only had a bare-bones contract. I paid him 20 percent up front for supplies. Midway through, he said he'd underestimated the job, so I agreed to pay him more. When he pulled this again toward the end of the job, I refused to pay. So he walked off, leaving me with half our roof gone. At this point I had withheld only 5 percent of the job costs. I decided it would be less costly in the long run to simply pay him what he asked and just get the job over with. Next time I'll be sure to get an airtight contract and withhold at least 20 percent as a final payment. And I would never again hire a friend—business and pleasure definitely do not mix when it comes to renovation.

Paul B., Nashua, New Hampshire

being your own contractor

Consider carefully before you DIY

You may find yourself wondering why you need a contractor in the first place. After all, it's not as if he'll be doing any building. How hard can it be to act as your own contractor?

Acting as your own general contractor will certainly save you money. How much? Most contractors take the cost of materials and labor and add 20 to 30 percent. This can be a significant savings.

But taking on the role of contractor is not a decision to make lightly. How big is your project? Overseeing the remodeling of existing space will be easier than supervising new construction.

Take an honest look at yourself beforehand. Do you have a complete understanding of your project and a good grasp of the construction process? Can you read a blueprint? Handle hiring subcontractors?

Are you organized? You'll need to schedule appropriate tradespeople and apply for permits and inspections.

Will you be available to be on site or at least on call while the work is going on? Do you take problems in stride? Remember that almost no renovation is glitch-free. If something goes wrong, you'll be the one to deal with it.

Will you be able to stay the course? Contractors don't like to take over a job in progress, particularly that of a nonprofessional, because of the potential work involved in correcting mistakes. And remember that you get no labor warranty, because you're the one doing the labor.

If you feel you're up to the job, be sure to get appropriate insurance, such as builder's risk. Check with the agent who handles your homeowner's policy to find out exactly what you need and how much it will cost.

Ask the Experts

Can I do some of my own work during the renovation?

There's something satisfying about putting your own sweat equity into your home. Before you do, evaluate which jobs you're capable of handling. If you're a beginner, your best bet is to try your hand at some of the finishing work, which is work done after major construction is complete, such as painting or adding decorative moldings. Or you can tackle demolition, such as tearing out cabinets and flooring. Just be sure that your back can handle it!

If you do choose to do the labor for a part of your renovation, be sure to specify this fact to your contractor so he doesn't include the price of that labor in the bid.

I designed and want to build a modern-looking guest cottage, but our local zoning ordinances forbid modern additions to historic properties like mine. What can I do?

If your project goes against any zoning ordinances, you can apply for a **variance**: an exception from zoning regulations granted by your local building department. The process for getting a variance varies by town. You may have to meet with an official, defend your exception before a board, or get the approval of your neighbors or other parties.

If your plans go against building codes, things get more complicated. There are international codes, regional codes, and local codes. You could very well get a variance that excepts you from a local code, especially if it's an appearance issue, but other structural changes (e.g. a noncode staircase or window) may be harder to get approved. A lot has to do with the age of your house and whether there are any grandfather laws regarding it. If you live in a historic house or neighborhood or a planned community, your renovation is likely to be subject to even more restrictions and bureaucracy than usual.

Go with the pros

Anything that involves your home's systems (electric, plumbing, heating) is best left to a professional. You don't want hot water pouring onto your basement floor or your circuits blown, nor do you want to injure yourself. Don't install appliances before reading the manufacturer's warranty carefully. Some warranties are voided if the item isn't installed by a licensed professional.

now what do I do?

Answers to common questions

Should I tell my neighbors I'm remodeling?

Informing your neighbors can do a lot to keep relationships smooth during what may be a trying time for everyone. Let them know the start and completion dates, and if there are days they may have difficulty parking, or when the noise could be at its worst. They may appreciate your openness and honesty and pay you back by opening their homes to you for much-needed remodeling breaks.

What happens if I forego getting a permit?

Getting a permit isn't a choice, it's a necessity. Building codes and permits exist for a reason. They're there to protect you from unscrupulous contractors and shoddy workmanship. A building that's not up to code can be hazardous to live in. If your town finds out you're doing a renovation and didn't apply for a permit, they can levy a fine or even make you tear out the work and redo it at your expense.

My friend tells me I should never sign for deliveries. Why not?

You'll be putting your signature on a lot of paperwork during a renovation, but never sign for materials delivered to your home unless you ordered them personally. If the contractor doesn't pay for the materials, the vendor will come after you for payment. And there's always the possibility that the supplies weren't even for your job! Best to let the contractor handle accepting and inspecting shipments.

Is it a good idea to include a late-penalty clause?

A late-penalty clause holds the contractor financially responsible for delays. It's a good way to ensure your contractor won't be goofing off rather than working. On the other hand, you wouldn't want him to cut corners because the work is running behind schedule. Make sure to set a reasonable deadline. A word of advice: It's not a good idea to schedule your remodeling's completion date too close to an important event you plan to celebrate in your home, such as Thanksgiving or your daughter's wedding. You'd be beside yourself wondering if the project would get done on time, and more stress is the last thing you need!

I'm interviewing a contractor who grew up in the community, has worked for a lot of customers, and is a member of the local church and PTA. Why should I go nuts performing background checks and insisting on a contract with so many provisions?

This contractor could be talented, honest, and hardworking. But there are still a lot of things you don't know. He may not be doing well financially and could declare bankruptcy midway through your project. He could have been padding his bids with charges that none of his other customers caught on to until the end of their projects, and they may have filed complaints at your local building department. If the contractor is a true professional, he'll understand that business is business, and that you will need to research his work history and put together an ironclad contract. If he seems hurt or just assures you everything will be okay and not to worry, wish him the best and find someone else.

Now where do I go?

BOOKS

Renovation Style magazine

Outwitting Contractors: The Complete Guide to Surviving Your Home or Apartment Renovation
by Bill Adler, Jr.

Hiring Contractors Without Going Through Hell: How to Find, Hire, Supervise, and Pay Professional Help for Home Renovations and Repairs
by Ellis Levinson

The Homeowners' Guide to Hiring Contractors: How to Save Time, Money and Headaches by Hiring the Right Contractor for Your Job
by Brett P. Kennelly with Eddy Hall

WEB SITES

The American Institute of Architects
www.aia.org

The American Society of Interior Designers
www.asid.org

The American Arbitration Association
www.adr.org

The Design/Build Institute of America
www.dbia.org

The National Association of the Remodeling Industry
www.nari.org

The National Kitchen and Bath Association
www.nkba.org

Chapter 3

Kitchens

kitchen improvements

Pairing function with design

So you're planning to remodel your kitchen. You certainly have plenty of company! Only the bathroom is as popular when it comes to remodeling. An up-to-date, well-planned kitchen can pay back a good percentage of your renovation costs when you sell your home (see pages 12–13).

Renovating a kitchen can be a daunting task. Your kitchen packs a lot of function into one room. It's where you cook, bake, brew coffee, heat up leftovers in the microwave, wash dirty dishes, and dispose of trash. Your kitchen also needs to have plenty of storage space for cookware and dishes.

In addition to these functions, the kitchen may be where you prefer to eat, entertain, pay bills, or work on the computer. The kitchen could even be your true living room. These days, everything from sofas and televisions to stereos, desks, and computers are being included in kitchen remodels.

Kitchen designs run the gamut—from ultra-modern with professional appliances and stainless steel cabinets to rustic, country style with burled wood cabinets, beamed ceilings, and a farmhouse-style sink.

Unless the sky's the limit when it comes to money, you'll need to watch out for budget busters like hardwood floors, granite countertops, custom cabinets, and commercial-grade appliances. But do give yourself some room to splurge. An eye-catching lighting fixture, a Victorian-style faucet, or even whimsical decorative drawer pulls and door handles are the little touches that really personalize your kitchen.

PRIORITIZING DESIGN DECISIONS

Think about what you like and don't like about your kitchen and ask yourself these questions to settle on a plan for your remodel.

Are you unhappy with its looks? You can lay down a vinyl floor, reface the cabinets, replace countertops, and paint or wallpaper. These simple changes are much less expensive than full kitchen remodels.

Do you want new appliances? Keeping your old appliances can save money, but you may be missing out on better energy efficiency or helpful new features such as sealed burners for easy cleaning.

Is the layout inconvenient? Can two people prepare meals at once without getting in each other's way? A more efficient layout usually means a new floor and cabinets, repainting or wallpapering, and a lot of measuring and planning.

Does the kitchen feel too walled in? Today's kitchens are often open to the dining room, family room, or both. Consult an architect or engineer and find out if it's safe to remove walls (see page 15).

Is the kitchen too small? Maybe you can steal space from an adjacent area, add windows, or raise the ceiling. Extending the kitchen outward is another option, and it can be cheaper than relocating your kitchen to another area, which requires a new plumbing stack and pipes, ventilation ducts, and possibly gas lines.

kitchen layouts

The all-important work triangle

Common kitchen layouts

When planning your kitchen, consider these five typical kitchen layouts and imagine how your work triangle could be set up within it.

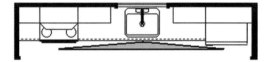

One wall Instead of a triangle, you have one component on each end of the wall and one in the middle. If space is at a premium, this layout may be your only choice.

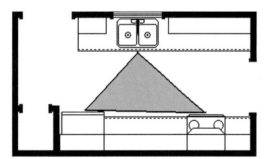

Galley Two parallel walls, with two points of the triangle on one wall and one on the opposite. Only caters to one cook and contains no eating area, although it can be adjacent to one.

Kitchen design is based on a simple concept that truly works—the work triangle. Creating a good work triangle reduces footsteps and thus increases efficiency. To do it, make one point of the triangle the sink, one the refrigerator, and the third the cooking area. Make the three points equidistant, with each side four to nine feet long.

The work triangle theory may not cut it if your kitchen is very large and busy. In this case, think in terms of work centers: two or more triangles that fill different functions. Your kitchen can include work centers for cooking, cleanup, paperwork, or anything else.

Here's an example of work centers in action. Imagine that you're preparing dinner using the refrigerator, stove, and sink. Meanwhile, your children are getting milk out of the fridge and cookies out of the cabinet and eating them at the snack bar—without getting under your feet! How is this possible? Their snack center overlaps your cooking center a little, because both use the refrigerator, but the rest of the snack center uses its own counter space and cabinets, so your children can have their snacks without getting in your way.

Ask the Experts

Where do I even begin laying out my kitchen?

Start with your sink as the first point in your triangle, since placement is dependent on your plumbing connection. The dishwasher should be no more than 36 inches from the sink, since it shares that all-important plumbing line, and because dishes and pots travel from sink to dishwasher. Then slot in your main cooking appliances and refrigerator. Fill spaces in between with cabinets, counter space, and windows. Last, place an island or eating area.

Is there any way to make kitchen planning easier?

Here's a helpful hint: Buy a simple design kit—some come packaged with kitchen remodeling books. You get a graph paper grid and cutout templates of kitchen appliances and cabinetry in standard sizes. Explore layouts by arranging the templates to your heart's content. Kind of like a dollhouse for grown-ups! You can also use a computer design program (see page 23).

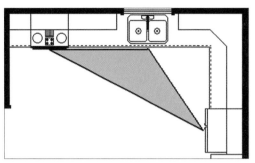

L-shaped Two adjacent walls joined at a right angle. There is more working room and the ability to incorporate an island or peninsula.

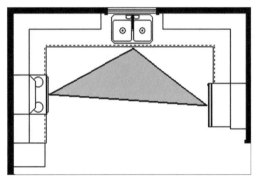

U-shaped Two parallel and one joining them. This shape offers the most room for storage and counter space. It can also accommodate two cooks.

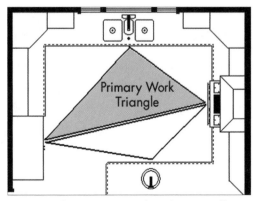

G-shaped This variation on the U has a small "leg" in the form of a breakfast nook or island.

the eat-in kitchen

Tables, booths, and banquettes

You've no doubt seen the abbreviation "EIK" (eat-in kitchen) pop up an awful lot in real estate ads. Many of us prefer to eat and even socialize in the kitchen, rather than in a formal dining room. If you are planning an eating area as part of your kitchen remodel, consider how many people you'll be serving, how you want to serve them, and what space is available.

The most common choice for serving informal meals in your kitchen is a freestanding table and chairs. In many homes, the kitchen table is situated in an area officially termed the "breakfast nook." You have a wide choice of table and chair styles to suit your kitchen's décor and your family's comfort.

If space doesn't allow for a table and chairs, there are other options. You can place your table in front of a window seat or banquette (an upholstered, built-in bench), either of which can provide storage space underneath, and then set freestanding chairs on the other side. Built-in booths also maximize square footage by fitting in tight corners or other spaces that would have gone to waste.

A bump-out (see page 15) is sometimes all that's needed in a kitchen to provide space for a banquette, table, or window seat, not to mention bring in more light with a sunny bay window.

You can also add counter space for eating in the form of an island or peninsula. Vary the heights so that one side is 36 inches high for food prep and the other is bar height, 42 inches, for sitting. You may even want to have two eating areas in your kitchen: a table or banquette for meals plus a snack-bar counter area.

Ask the Experts

How much space do I need for various eating areas?

For a table and chairs, figure that each person needs a square of floor space that's at least 3 by 3 feet and an area of table space in front of them that's 21 to 24 inches wide. Leave 44 inches of clearance space around each side of the table for people to move around. A booth or banquette needs a 12-inch clearance between seat and tabletop, and seats should be 18 inches off the ground. For an island snack bar, set the counters at bar height, about 42 inches, not the standard 36-inch height that's comfortable for standing. Allow 24 inches underneath for knee space.

What exactly is the difference between a booth and a banquette?

A banquette is a built-in upholstered bench that is straight, L-shaped, or U-shaped. You can put a table in front of it and chairs on the other side of the table to create a small eating area. A booth is like the booths you find in a diner. You have two built-in benches with a built-in table between them.

What can I do if I have very little space in my kitchen but would like to include an eating area?

You can have a table custom-built to fit into an awkward space, such as a triangular shape to fit into a corner or a semicircle to fit against a wall. If you dine in your kitchen infrequently, you can use a folding table and chairs that can be closed up and stored, say, between the wall and the refrigerator. Keep in mind that these tables can only comfortably seat two people.

kitchen islands and peninsulas

One stop for food preparation, eating, and storage

Tired of facing the wall while you chop and wash vegetables at the counter? Add a kitchen island or peninsula. Two of the most popular kitchen amenities today, these units can provide counter, seating, and storage space in one compact area. They also keep your kitchen open to other rooms while providing just that little bit of separation between them.

A kitchen island has four unattached sides, while a peninsula is attached at a right angle to a wall or cabinet bank. Both islands and peninsulas are usually fixed to the floor, but they can be freestanding too.

Your island or peninsula can offer just a simple, flat surface for food prep, but it can also be incredibly versatile in terms of configuration. You can have a standard-height countertop on one side for food prep and a higher counter on the other for seated bar-style eating. Your island can also include a small sink or cooktop. You may also want to include an electrical outlet and appropriate lighting over the island.

What about underneath? You can use shelving in this area to store cookbooks or cookware, show off a collection, or house a microwave or dishwasher.

Because they offer so much function in a small space, you can perform many tasks at your island or peninsula without having to waste footsteps moving around the kitchen. Remember to make sure there are 42 inches of space around the island and other work surfaces to allow you to open cabinet and appliance doors easily and to help traffic flow smoothly.

Ask the Experts

Can I install a sink and a cooktop in my island?

Yes, but there's more than meets the eye here. A sink needs plumbing lines and a gas cooktop needs a gas line. A cooktop also requires ventilation, so you'll need to include an overhead unit or downdraft, with a vent line routed to an exterior outlet. Running pipes and ducts shouldn't be a problem if you have a basement, but this is much more difficult to do if your ground floor is constructed on a concrete slab foundation. A peninsula would be a better choice here, since one side is connected to a wall, through which you can run pipes if necessary. And keep in mind that if you have a sink and outlet, most codes require that your island or peninsula be anchored to the floor.

Do islands have to be rectangular?

Definitely not. They can be round, oval, oblong, crescent-shaped, or even octagonal. An island can even be circular, with room to stand inside it. Keep in mind that the more inventive the shape, the more you may have to pay for it.

What can I do if I can't afford a built-in island or peninsula?

A freestanding island is a less expensive option. Or try a kitchen cart. These units are usually on wheels and constructed of wood or wire with a butcher block, stone, or laminate counter surface. Carts are usually smaller than islands, but their mobility can make them more versatile. Some carts have drop leaves for extra working space and storage racks. You can find freestanding islands and carts at Web sites like **www.kitchencarts.com** or **www.kitchenislands.com**. A sturdy wood farmhouse-style worktable is another option, although the table height will be more comfortable for sitting than for standing food prep.

cabinets

A big chunk of your kitchen budget

Cabinets are pivotal to the look and function of your kitchen, as well as an important part of your remodeling budget. Luckily, there are cabinets in all price ranges. And if new cabinets are more than your budget can handle, you can always update your existing ones by repainting them, adding new doors, or changing the handles.

Wood—typically maple, oak, or cherry—is the most popular choice for cabinet doors, and imparts a warm, natural look. The type of finish applied can greatly affect the color and characteristics of the wood. These cabinets may also have embellishments like gingerbread, fretwork, pilasters, or molding on top. The boxes, or carcasses, are usually made of a durable material like plywood, fiberboard, or particleboard.

Framed cabinets

You can also go for laminate or metal cabinets. These are economical choices and come in a range of colors. Stainless-steel cabinets are considerably more expensive but will give your kitchen a modern, high-tech, professional appearance.

Cabinets come in myriad shapes and forms. **Framed cabinets** leave the box frame around the door exposed for a more traditional look, and they may also have ornamentation. The doors of **frameless cabinets** cover the box frame. These are usually free of ornamentation, creating a more contemporary look.

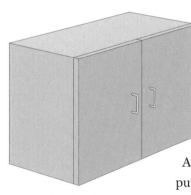

Frameless cabinets

Cabinets are also available in several levels of customization. At the low end are ready-to-assemble, or **RTA cabinets**, which you put together yourself. Then there are **stock cabinets**, which come in standard sizes and different styles. With semicustom cabinets, you choose stock sizes, then select a door style, color, and finish; these are usually delivered in about eight weeks.

You can also order **custom cabinets** from a cabinetmaker. However, you'll pay for the expertise: Custom cabinets typically cost 30 to 50 percent more than semicustom ones. Plus, you may have to wait up to 20 weeks to get them. You can cut costs, however, by ordering just one custom unit to complement stock cabinets.

CABINET ACCESSORIES

Cabinet designers are constantly coming up with innovative accessories and options to make cabinets even more efficient. Because cabinets and accessories are meant to work together, it's best to find one manufacturer for all your cabinet needs. Some of these accessories may need to be dropped into the base cabinets before the countertop is installed, so don't let them become an afterthought.

Shelving You have many options when it comes to shelving. A rustic country cabinet door can conceal ingenious carousels and wire dividers. Tracking systems will enable you to adjust the height of individual shelves. Narrow, vertical space between cabinets can contain a pullout wire pantry unit.

Storage If you don't like the unsightly look of appliances cluttering your countertop, consider making one cabinet into an appliance garage. As the name implies, you park your food processor or coffee maker inside, and hide it from view until you need it. Make sure the garage contains an electrical outlet. You can also put the toe kick (the area underneath your base cabinets) to good use by adding wide, shallow drawers for flat items like dishtowels, baking sheets, or newspaper for recycling.

Accessories Pullout cutting boards give you extra cutting space when you need it, and then disappear into a slot. Outfit awkward corner cabinet space with a carousel that rotates 270 degrees, or a lazy Susan that turns 360 degrees.

floor coverings

Balancing looks, cost, and maintenance

Flooring greatly affects how a kitchen looks. Like walls and ceilings, floors cover a large expanse. But unlike the other two, floors take a lot of wear and tear. For this reason, you should pick flooring that combines practicality with a style that complements your kitchen design.

An unusual color or pattern on the floor makes a statement, but can also steal the spotlight from the rest of your décor. A simple, uniform floor will gently recede into the background and let other elements of the room take center stage. Using the same flooring in adjoining rooms creates visual coherence and continuity, while using different flooring defines separate areas.

When choosing flooring, think about how the room will be used. Flooring differs in its durability, maintenance requirements, and feel. Stone and tile are extremely durable, but cold on bare feet (unless you install radiant hot-water heat or electric heat beneath them; see page 90). They are also hard on the legs if you stand on them for long periods, and slippery and unforgiving if you take a spill or drop a glass. That's an important consideration if your family includes children or people who are elderly or disabled.

Flooring materials also vary widely in price. Laminates and resilient flooring are often the cheapest options, followed by hardwood and tile, with stone being the most expensive. But a quality vinyl floor can cost as much as some hard-

A Vinyl sheet
B Ceramic porcelain tile

woods. Today's vinyl and laminate floors can also closely mimic the look of wood, stone, or tile.

And don't forget to consider the cost of labor. Some floors can be laid over your existing floor, while others will require having your old floor removed. The condition of your subfloor can also increase labor costs. Consult the dealer, manufacturer, or your contractor before choosing a flooring type. The World Floor Covering Association (**www.wfca.org**) offers in-depth information on flooring types and installation.

A GUIDE TO FLOORING MATERIALS

Laminate flooring stands up well to spills and household wear, is inexpensive, and typically lasts 10 to 20 years. It's popular in kitchens, baths, and playrooms. Manufacturers include Pergo (**www.pergo.com**) and Wilsonart (**www.wilsonart.com**).

Resilient flooring includes vinyl, linoleum, rubber, and cork. These floors are inexpensive, easy to install and maintain, and soft underfoot. Often used in kitchens, bathrooms, and playrooms, these floors can last 20 to 30 years. Manufacturers include Armstrong (**www.armstrongfloors.com**) and Congoleum (**www.congoleum.com**).

Hardwood is easy on the feet and long-lasting, but susceptible to moisture damage, so it may not be the best choice for kitchens, bathrooms, or basements. Most woods are coated with polyurethane to protect them from wear and tear, and are available in various finishes. Costs are moderate to high, depending on the type of wood. A major supplier is Bruce Hardwood.

Ceramic tile is available in a range of colors, patterns, shapes, and finishes that can be combined for a decorative effect. Glazed tile is less porous than unglazed and offers protection against stains. Tile, which requires an extra-strength subfloor, is a popular choice for kitchens and bathrooms and holds up well, although the grout may need replacing periodically. Choose a darker grout that won't show dirt.

Stone includes marble, granite, limestone, and flagstone. Sealing is necessary to prevent stains, and the weight requires a strong subfloor. Popular in kitchens, bathrooms, and foyers, stone gives a luxurious look and is very durable, but you'll pay a high price for it. Both ceramic tile and stone are harder on the feet than other flooring materials.

kitchen lighting

Illuminating food prep and dining

With all the other things you have to think about during a kitchen remodel, you may forget to plan the lighting in advance. Don't. Proper lighting is a must in a room where so many activities take place and where safety is a concern.

If you want to add windows, first be sure to check out the view you will have. Then consider the **exposure**, or amount and type of natural light the kitchen receives:

- East windows let in early morning light and can make the morning rush more bearable.

- West windows bring in late afternoon light that is pleasant for when you're making dinner or winding down from the day.

- A southern exposure lets in the most light but also the most heat.

- A northern view offers less direct, cooler-toned light.

Next, plan your ambient lighting—generally from a ceiling fixture. A fluorescent fixture offers the most light for the lowest cost, but you can also choose track lighting, which consists of individual, adjustable lighting heads mounted in a row, or recessed lighting. Or try a combination ceiling fan and light, which provides both light and air circulation.

The lighting you choose will affect your energy bills. Incandescent bulbs provide a warm-toned, flattering light, but require more energy and don't last as long as fluorescent or halogen bulbs. Fluorescent lights are the most energy efficient. They've come a long way from the buzzing, bluish-cast bulbs of years ago. They're quieter now, and the light they emit is whiter in tone and more closely resembles incandescent light or natural sunlight. For more lighting tips, contact the American Lighting Association (**www.ala.org**).

KITCHEN TASK LIGHTING

As you plan your kitchen remodel, think about specific areas that will require task lighting. The larger the kitchen, the more additional lighting you'll need:

■ Under cabinets. You need good task lighting here, especially if this is where you'll be doing food prep. Slim fluorescent lights and miniature track lights that affix to cabinet bottoms work well.

■ Over the sink. Fixtures such as recessed down lights on a separate switch let you see what you're doing when washing up.

■ Over the range. Make sure the area over the stove is lit. Many range hoods contain light fixtures for this purpose, or you can use a fluorescent strip or recessed down lights.

■ Over the kitchen table. A hanging decorative pendant is sufficient for this area. Put it on a dimmer switch to adjust the mood when you move from work to dining.

■ Over an island. Hanging pendants or track lighting provide task lighting for when you're working at the island.

■ Inside cabinets. Small fixtures can help out by letting you see what's inside a dark cabinet.

ACCENT LIGHTING

Use accent lighting to highlight specific features of your kitchen, such as decorative moldings or a prized collection. Lighting over cabinets, aimed indirectly at the ceiling, can brighten up dark corners and make your kitchen appear more spacious.

countertops

Materials for all budgets and preferences

When you go countertop shopping, think of the surface you'd most like to work at and what style or color will complement your kitchen decor. Consider each material's properties, and remember to keep an eye on the price tag, as countertop materials can vary widely in cost. Here are some materials to consider:

■ Plastic laminate is available in a variety of colors and patterns and is waterproof and stain-resistant, but it can be scratched by sharp knives or scorched by a hot pot. It can't be patched, so if damaged, the whole countertop will need to be replaced.

Corian

■ Ceramic tile is durable and, if glazed, is resistant to scratches, burns, and stains. Tile is available in a myriad of colors and patterns, and you can mix and match to create unique designs. Tile must be regrouted periodically. White grout can show stains, so you may want to choose a darker color.

■ Wood is beloved for its warmth and beauty, but it expands and contracts with temperature changes and warps when damp. A varnish or lacquer finish can help, but you'll have to reseal it annually.

■ Stone is extremely long lasting, but it's one of the most expensive options. Choices include granite, soapstone, limestone, slate, engineered quartz, and even concrete. Stone is heatproof, waterproof, and (in the case of concrete) can be cut or molded to fit, but it can chip. Natural stone must be sealed to protect against staining and scratching. Engineered stone does not require sealing.

■ Stainless steel is heatproof, waterproof, noncorrosive, and hygienic. The only drawbacks: It's expensive and can scratch easily.

■ Solid surfacing material (such as DuPont's Corian) is durable, waterproof, heat resistant, and easy to clean. It also comes in a variety of colors and edge treatments. However, you'll pay for all these features, as this material rivals stone in cost.

Ask the Experts

My husband, who is six feet four, is uncomfortable working at a standard kitchen countertop. My seven-year-old wants to help out too. What can we do?

Vary your countertop heights. The standard counter height is 36 inches off the ground. Taller people may be more comfortable with 37 inches or higher, while a 30-inch-high counter provides better access for children. A stool or built-in sliding step under the toe kick can also be used by children or smaller adults to bring them up to counter height.

I have my heart set on stone counters, but there's no way I can afford them. Any ideas?

Use it judiciously. There's certainly no rule specifying that you have to choose one countertop material and stick to it. You can use one material near the stove, another near the sink, and a third on an island or peninsula. A stone insert, rather than full stone counters, can be an attractive and less expensive option. If you like to bake, place it near the oven and use it for rolling pastry.

FIRST PERSON DISASTER STORY
Communication breakdown

My big remodeling splurge was a granite countertop. I picked out the perfect slab, had it installed, and immediately started working at it. I had been assured that the granite couldn't be scratched or stained, so imagine my surprise when I noticed a blueberry stain that wouldn't come out! Essentially, my designer and contractor had each assumed that the other person had explained to me that granite needs to be sealed for protection before you can work on it. Luckily, they gave me instructions for making a poultice to remove the stain, which finally did the trick after a few applications. And, of course, I applied the sealant before using the counter again.

Dana F., Sioux Falls, South Dakota

sinks and faucets

Combining form and function

Let's face it, we all spend a lot of kitchen time standing over the sink. It simply makes sense to purchase a sink and faucet that meet your needs, are a pleasure to use, and add an attractive element to your kitchen.

Sink and faucet showrooms are packed with options, but don't be lured too much by looks. Expensive materials and artistic interpretations can drive up the price of sinks and faucets substantially. Function is more important. After all, there's nothing more annoying than a leaky faucet, a hard-to-clean sink, or a basin that's too small for soaking large pots.

Single-lever faucet

Because it's durable and easy to clean, stainless steel is the most popular sink material. If you dislike the metallic look, you can opt instead for a steel or cast-iron sink coated with decorative enamel, but beware—the coating can chip. **Solid surfacing material**, cast iron, and quartz composite are other popular options.

You also need to think about the size and number of bowls or basins you will need. Deep bowls make it easier to clean large pots and pans. A double- or triple-basin sink lets you keep rinsed vegetables separate from soaking dishes.

Next up: faucets. Most of today's models are washerless, making them less prone to leaks and longer lasting than washer varieties. A chrome faucet is the least expensive. Going up the price scale you'll find other materials like nickel, pewter, and brass.

If you want a faucet that's a little different, get one with a spout that can be pulled out for targeted cleaning or a **gooseneck faucet**, which is tall and arched, providing clearance for large pots. You can also have separate valves for hot and cold water or a single lever that connects to the spout for one-handed operation.

Ask the Experts

How can I possibly choose between all the different types of sinks?

You may not have to. More and more kitchens feature two different sinks—for example, a main, deep-bowled sink in the work triangle for washing pots and a smaller sink in an island for rinsing food. If having two sinks isn't a possibility, you can make your sink more versatile by using inexpensive accessories. Use clip-on drain boards for drying dishes and clip-on colander baskets and cutting boards for holding rinsed vegetables or chopping food over the sink.

I have a boring blank wall behind my sink. What are some ideas for jazzing it up a bit?

The wall that runs from behind your sink to the bottom of the wall cabinets is called the backsplash, and derives its name from the fact that it protects the wall from splashing water. Unlike larger wall and floor areas, the backsplash is a great way to make a bit of a "splash" design-wise, because new owners can easily replace it if you decide to sell your house. While most backsplashes are covered with ceramic wall tile, other choices include glass wall tile, stone, and stainless steel. For an even more distinctive look, add a window above your sink (that is, if the view outside is nice) and design your backsplash to complement it.

Gooseneck faucet

appliances 101

A staggering choice
of styles, sizes, bells,
and whistles

After you've completed the structural basics, it's time to think about kitchen appliances. Upgrading your appliances will have a huge impact on how your kitchen functions, never mind your budget.

Before you do anything, consider the age of your current appliances. No appliance lasts forever. If an older model is reaching the end of its lifetime, around 15 to 20 years, this may be a good time to replace it. Even 10-year-old appliances may not be as energy efficient as newer models, which can save you money by cutting down your electric bills. If you haven't visited an appliance store for a few years, you'll be amazed at how appliances have changed and how many new features are available.

If you've decided to invest in new appliances, think hard about what kind and what size you need. Don't just think about your life as it is now; look a few years ahead. Will your kitchen be used for lots of cooking and entertaining? Are you starting a family? Or will your children be out of the house in a few years?

In addition to major appliances, think about what other appliances you'd like and where you'd want to put them. Including a built-in shelf for your microwave will put it at eye level and free up counter space. What about small appliances like food processors, blenders, and toaster ovens? Think about how many you use and how often you use them. If you rarely use these appliances, you may not want them cluttering the countertop on an everyday basis.

SHOPPING FOR APPLIANCES

Your appliances are the workhorses of your home. Don't be swayed too much by looks and fancy features. Performance and durability are far more important. Remember, you'll probably be living with these guys for at least 10 years! Here are some tips to make shopping easier:

1. Do your research Buy consumer magazines that rate models by brand, such as *Consumer Reports*. Many manufacturers' Web sites provide in-depth specifications on different models, so you may be able to download the manuals of appliances you're interested in purchasing (or ask a dealer for them).

2. Keep it simple Don't blow your budget on bells and whistles you'll never use. The world's fanciest oven or range won't turn you into a gourmet chef.

3. Save your energy Energy efficiency is one quality that's worth paying extra for. Manufacturers must label each item with a yellow Energy Guide; these tags show you projected energy costs for the item as well as how it compares to similar models in energy efficiency.

4. Don't forget mechanical requirements A ducted ventilation system requires vents. Gas appliances need gas lines. A refrigerator with a water dispenser needs a water line. Factor in these costs when you plan.

5. Check the warranty Ask plenty of questions about what it covers and for how long. Some warranties cover the entire unit for one period and then offer extended protection only for specific components. And always check the warranty before you install an appliance yourself. Some warranties are voided if a licensed professional does not install the unit.

6. Find out what's included Ask whether delivery and installation are included in the price of the appliance.

refrigerators and stoves

The appliances you can't live without

You may not cook much, but there are two appliances that just about every house has: a refrigerator and a stove. There are many things to consider when you're in the market for these appliances.

When shopping for a refrigerator, first think about how much you need to store in it. A general rule is to start with 12 cubic feet of total refrigerator/freezer space for two people and then add 2 cubic feet for each additional family member.

Next, decide on the refrigerator's configuration: top-mount (freezer cabinet on top), bottom-mount (slide-out freezer drawer on bottom), or the more expensive side-by-side model. Also consider any special features you'd like, such as separate temperature and humidity controls or a water and ice dispenser in the door.

When it comes to a stove, your can choose gas, electric, or both (a unit with an electric oven and gas burners), and whether you want your oven and burners (also referred to as a cooktop) to be separate or combined in one unit. A separate oven and cooktop allows you more flexibility in terms of placement. And with a separate oven installed at eye level, you can check on what's cooking and take food in and out without bending over.

Whether separate or part of a unit, cooktops can include oversize burners, as well as griddles, deep fryers, or grills. Both electric and gas cooktops are available with sealed burners that keep spills away from the heating element.

Ovens can be conventional, convection, microwave—or any combination of these three. Conventional ovens contain one heating element for baking and roasting and one for broiling, while convection ovens, though noisier, circulate heated air for faster, more even cooking. A microwave is not essential, though it's handy for reheating food quickly. How about separate warming drawers? They can be installed in cabinet space and keep foods warm for long periods.

Ask the Experts

What other cooling appliances can I choose from besides the typical refrigerator/freezer unit?

If you're a wine connoisseur but don't have space for a wine cellar, try a wine cooler. They range in size and can store between 17 and 100 bottles of wine at 48°F to 60°F. You might also go for refrigerator and freezer drawers that are separate pullout units neatly hidden away in your cabinets, which allow you to store cold foods in different locations in your kitchen. You can adjust the temperature and humidity of each drawer.

I am planning a vintage kitchen and can't bear the thought of staring at that huge expanse of modern refrigerator. What can I do?

If the modern look isn't for you, your cabinet manufacturer might be able to provide you with appliance panels: wood panels that match your cabinetry and are installed on the appliance's door. Just make sure to purchase appliances that will accept these panels—one example is General Electric's Monogram collection (**www.monogram.com**). Or try Elmira Stove Works (**www.elmirastoveworks.com**), which sells appliances that look vintage but have most modern features. Another trick: Black appliances recede into the background and thus are less obtrusive.

What's the difference between self-cleaning, manual-cleaning, and continuous-cleaning ovens?

A manual-cleaning oven means you get out the oven cleaner, roll up your sleeves, and go to work. A self-cleaning oven, as the name implies, cleans itself. You still have to switch the oven to cleaning mode and set aside about three hours for the oven to heat itself up to roughly 900°F and burn off splatters. Continuous-cleaning ovens have a chemically treated finish that helps them burn off spills as they happen, at normal cooking temperatures. However, they tend not to work as well as self-cleaning ovens. Be aware that if you use an oven cleaning product on a continuous-cleaning oven, this can ruin its cleaning ability, and may even void the warranty.

> **Tip**
>
> Make sure to locate the refrigerator where there is room enough for someone to pass by when the door is open.

dishwashers and garbage disposals

The key to keeping your kitchen tidy

Dishwashers and garbage disposals are your kitchen's clean-up crew. Both should be near the sink—the garbage disposal should be under it, and the dishwasher no more than 36 inches away.

If you haven't shopped for a dishwasher in a while, you're in for a surprise. Dishwashers are a lot more energy efficient than they were a few years ago, and perform a lot better too. Washing a full load of dishes by hand or in an older unit used to take up to 16 gallons of water, while most of today's dishwashers use less than half that amount. They're also quieter due to better sound insulation around the drum. If you detest prerinsing dishes before loading them into the dishwasher, you can buy a model with a hard-food disposal that eliminates this chore.

Garbage disposal

The cleaning performance of your dishwasher depends on the number of wash arms. Basic models have one wash arm, while some high-end models have four. Capacity refers to how much you can load into the dishwasher. Most dishwashers hold 10 to 14 five-piece place settings, though if you need more, you can find a dishwasher with a larger capacity. Another trend is to have two dishwashers for faster cleanup after parties. You can use the extra dishwasher to store dinnerware when not in use.

Cycle options let you set the performance level so that you can do a heavy wash for plates or pans with baked-on food or a delicate cycle for fine china.

A garbage disposal grinds up food waste and flushes it through a waste line into the sewer. However, not all models can be used with septic systems. You'll also need to make sure your municipality allows the use of these units. You can choose either a batch-feed disposal that's activated via a built-in switch when you replace the drain lid, or a continuous-feed unit controlled by a wall switch.

Ask the Experts

What are some of the newest features for dishwashers?

Where shall we begin? There are dishwashers with three racks instead of the usual two, and some with racks you can move around in order to accommodate large pots and pans on the bottom and smaller items on top. Some models let you run a top-wash-only cycle for those times when you have a lot of dirty glasses but no plates. Others contain pressure sensors that adjust the water levels and cycle times according to the number of dishes and the amount of soiling involved. Hate tripping over the dishwasher door? Try a model that pulls out like a drawer instead.

I've heard that my area has hard water that could damage my new dishwasher. Will installing a water softener help?

It should. Hard water contains calcium and magnesium that can damage dishwashers, washing machines, and water heaters, not to mention plumbing pipes and your own skin (hard water can aggravate problems such as excema). You can install a kitchen water softener under the kitchen sink that connects to your plumbing line. These contain special salts that replace the calcium and magnesium ions with sodium, resulting in softer water. These smaller water softeners typically cost between $300 and $500, while a whole-house one will cost significantly more and will not fit under the sink.

Appliances and electricity

In a kitchen with many appliances, how do you keep from blowing a fuse every time you turn on the microwave? Ask your electrician how many dedicated circuits (electrical lines separate from other systems and appliances) you should have. Your refrigerator usually gets its own dedicated circuit, as do other power-hungry appliances like washing machines, dishwashers, and air conditioners. But keep in mind that water and electricity don't mix, so make sure every kitchen outlet has a ground fault circuit interrupter (GFCI) device. Required by most building codes, these devices cut the power if there's a surge or if moisture is detected, and can save you from electric shock.

now what do I do?
Answers to common questions

What kind of professional should I hire to design my kitchen?

An experienced contractor can handle a simple kitchen design, but if you're extending or relocating the kitchen, hire an architect. Architects are required by most towns to design or approve plans that involve adding space or changing your home's structure or systems. If you're only redoing the layout or updating your kitchen's look, hire an interior designer or a certified kitchen designer. According to the National Kitchen and Bath Association, a kitchen designer's average fee is about $600, but this varies depending on your region and the scope of your renovation. The association (**www.nkba.org**) can help you find a certified kitchen designer in your area.

What do I need to know about kitchen ventilation when remodeling?

Adequate ventilation is a must for venting cooking odors, gas fumes, and excess moisture. Ducted systems are better than ductless systems, and use fans or blowers to draw air through a filter and vent it outside. An updraft range hood, which pulls air up, should be installed 21 to 30 inches directly above the stove. A downdraft system draws air under the floor. Some cooktops have their own downdraft systems, making them handy for use in islands. Consult your designer or contractor to find out how powerful your system needs to be. The Heating and Ventilation Institute (**www.hvi.org**) also offers information on proper kitchen ventilation.

What is a magnetic induction cooktop, and is it an affordable alternative to a gas or electric range?

This type of cooktop uses an electromagnetic field to generate heat directly in your cookware. The cooktop surface remains cool to the touch. It doesn't even have to resemble a typical stove; some cooktops look like ceramic tile. Be aware that you'll need to use steel, steel alloy, or iron cookware, not aluminum, and expect to pay about $3,000 for a magnetic induction unit.

Should I include laundry facilities in my kitchen?

The kitchen can be a logical choice for laundry, since your washing machine can tap right into the plumbing line. Just make sure you have the space in your kitchen for a washer and dryer to fit comfortably, and keep in mind that you'll have a noisy washer and dryer in a main living area, possibly competing against a convection oven, microwave, or dishwasher.

What types of wall treatments work best in the kitchen?

Your best bet is to use wall tile or laminate over the backsplash, stove, or any other areas that need to hold up to moisture and flying food scraps. For other wall areas, go for washable paint or wallpaper. Eggshell or semigloss latex paint handles washing well, as does oil-based paint. But be aware you'll have to close off the kitchen or vacate the house until the oil paint dries.

I read something in a magazine about the "unfitted kitchen." What is this?

An unfitted kitchen combines built-in cabinets from one or more manufacturers with freestanding pieces, such as a hutch, and open shelving to give the impression of a kitchen that has been put together over years, maybe even over generations. Ironically, despite the casual, pulled-together look, unfitted kitchens are often carefully planned by interior designers! It's a perfect look if you love antiques and flea market finds or like to decorate in an eclectic style. But keep in mind that the eclectic mix of units in an unfitted kitchen won't make use of wall and floor space as efficiently as a fitted kitchen's wall-to-wall cabinets.

Now where do I go?

BOOKS

Better Homes and Gardens: Kitchens: Your Guide to Planning and Remodeling

The Smart Approach to Kitchen Design
by Susan Maney

DK Home Design Workbooks: Kitchen
by Johnny Grey

WEB SITES

The National Kitchen and Bath Association
www.nkba.org

The National Appliance Manufacturers' Association
www.nama.org

Resilient Floor Covering Institute
www.rfci.com

The American Lighting Association
www.ala.org

Rutt Custom Cabinetry
www.rutt1.com

Kraftmaid Cabinets
www.kraftmaid.com

Whirlpool
www.whirlpool.com

General Electric
www.ge.com

Delta Faucets
www.deltafaucet.com

Kohler
www.kohler.com

Chapter 4

Bathrooms

adding or remodeling a bath

Assess your space

Indulging in a bathroom renovation? Lucky you. Like most people, you probably dream of having a well-appointed bath that functions like a luxurious personal spa—a place where you can let your cares melt away. Bet you can feel your muscles relax just thinking about that whirlpool bath. You'll be in that tub soon enough, but taking the plunge into bathroom remodeling requires some careful thought and planning first.

Maybe you dream of relocating your bathroom to the back of your house, where you can bathe while gazing out upon your garden. Before you start, though, you're going to have to think about something that's a lot less pretty than garden views and decorative tile—your plumbing.

That's because bathrooms need water and lots of it, and they get it through your home's various plumbing lines, which ultimately connect to the waste or soil stack, the primary waste line of your home, which connects to the sewer line or septic tank.

You want to locate your bathroom fixtures as close to this stack as possible. Sure, you can snake lengths of pipe to connect to it, but beyond a certain point you'll wind up with gurgling pipes and backed-up drains. The alternative is to add a new stack, and they don't come cheap. Materials and labor could run you several thousand dollars. You can probably think of better ways to spend your remodeling dollars than on a new plumbing stack!

Your best bet is either to expand your existing bathroom, possibly by grabbing space from an adjacent room or closet, or to add a new bathroom next to it or directly above or below.

If you're adding an upstairs bath or installing a heavy tub or stone floor, it's always a good idea to have a structural engineer check the strength of the floor frame—the wooden joists that support the sub-floor (typically a plywood sheet). The whole system may need to be reinforced to bear the extra weight.

Ask the Experts

Who can help me design my new bathroom?

Don't skimp when it comes to design help. An architect is your first stop for a bathroom addition or total remodel that involves changes to the room's structure or systems. A certified bath designer (CBD) is a good choice if you're taking footage from existing living space and not moving heating or plumbing lines. Be sure to hire a contractor who's experienced with bathroom remodels and will hire qualified subcontractors.

My designer keeps talking about "compartmentalizing" and "zoning" my bathroom. What is this?

"Zoning" is a popular trend in bath design. By separating or leaving space between "wet" areas like tubs and showers and "dry" areas—toilet, lavatory, and vanity—you can enable more than one person to use the bathroom at once. For example, you can enclose the toilet in a separate stall or enclosure, almost like what you'd find in a public bathroom, put a partition between toilet and tub, or raise the tub a few steps to create some separation. Zoning is a great idea if your family is open to sharing the bathroom at the same time, but it wouldn't work as well if you prefer more privacy.

master baths

**When bed and bath
are en suite**

The master bath is the superstar of the bathroom world—and the stuff that bathroom remodeling dreams are made of. It's where you can create a haven for indulging in fixtures like whirlpool tubs and steam showers. Master baths are getting larger, often featuring non-traditional amenities like sofas, fireplaces, entertainment systems, and exercise equipment.

If you want to enlarge or add a master bath, look for extra space you can use. Is there an adjacent room, hallway, or closet you're not using? If the answer is no, you may need to carve space out of the master bedroom itself; perhaps you can sacrifice a closet, for example.

If you and your spouse are going to be using the redesigned master bath, it's important to sit down and discuss preferences for the bathroom's appearance and function. Consider your bathing habits. Will you really have time to take a whirlpool bath if you're rarely home? Maybe what you really need are dual lavatories, mirrors, and vanities so you won't fight over bathroom time or trip over each other during the morning rush. Is bathing an activity you enjoy doing together, or is the bathroom where you like to enjoy a private interlude? How open should the master bath be to the bedroom?

Don't be upset if you find yourselves disagreeing. Many couples with large, luxury homes are foregoing the shared master bath in favor of his-and-hers bathrooms!

Ask the Experts

My girlfriend wants to put a minigym in our master bath. I've never heard of such a thing!

Don't be so surprised—today's baths truly can be multipurpose. Some double as media centers and have telephones, televisions, and sound systems. Some have a minifridge so you can grab a snack while watching a movie from the tub, or include a dressing area that connects to a walk-in closet. A bathroom also makes a terrific greenhouse for moisture-loving plants. And yes, an exercise area is another popular option. You can work out on a stationary bicycle or treadmill and then hop into a whirlpool tub to soothe your muscles!

How can I expand my master bath without losing my open, spacious bedroom?

If you have a standard bathroom door, replace it with a mirrored or glass door, or pocket doors that slide into the wall rather than swing in or out. Open them up and your bathroom will feel like part of your bedroom, then simply close the doors when you want more privacy. If you are more daring, put a tub and lavatory in a corner of the bedroom, then enclose the toilet in a separate room or a stall, similar to a public bathroom. Just make sure there is proper ventilation and that the flooring can hold up to water use.

Decorating tip

To visually unify the master bedroom and bath, keep color schemes and styles the same and use complementary wall treatments and flooring. Manufacturers of bedding and bath items—such as Wamsutta, Springmaid, and Waverly— often produce the same designs and patterns for both rooms, so you can have matching or color-coordinated bedding, window treatments, shower curtains, and bath accessories.

family baths

Safety and organization should be top priorities

The common depiction in magazines of the children's bath is that of a brightly tiled room, perhaps with a mural on the wall, and nary a stray bath toy in sight. In the real world, children's baths aren't always so storybook perfect. And if you don't have the luxury of a master bath, the family bath has to work that much harder to serve the needs of both children and adults.

Start by considering the number of people who will be using the bathroom, their ages, and their bathing habits. Most children under 10 prefer baths to showers. A tub with higher sides will keep splashes from soaking the floor. Will teenagers and adults who like showers also be using the bathroom? If you don't have space for a separate shower, install a combination tub/shower unit.

If you have children who must get ready for bed or school at the same time, consider adding a small partition between toilet and tub to give one child a little extra privacy while another child is bathing. Two lavatories make as much sense in this bath as they do in the master bathroom.

Provide a towel bar for each family member, as well as enough cabinets and storage space for everyone. Don't forget to include a shelf or cabinet for all the bath toys young children manage to collect. If the children are older, you'll need to devote plenty of storage to their grooming products.

Since the family bath gets so much use, faucets must be able to withstand a lot of turning, and flooring should be extra durable.

Ask the Experts

I have a two-year-old and a five-year-old. What safety features do I need to include in our family bathroom?

Install childproof locks on drawers and cabinets, especially those that store cleaning supplies or medications, or store these items out of the bathroom altogether. Use antiscald devices to prevent the water from getting too hot and thermostatic shower valves to enable you to set the temperature and water level. Stay away from tubs, lavatories, or vanities with sharp edges. A small stepstool, perhaps one personalized for each child, will help give your children a boost up to the sink and toilet. And remember that no matter how many safety features you include, don't ever leave a small child in the tub unattended. If you have some extra space, a comfortable chair for the attending grown-up will make bath time more enjoyable for everyone.

How can I decorate my daughter's bathroom in a way she'll like now but won't outgrow in a few years?

The trouble is that children often tire of themes and color schemes before you do. Unless you're planning on another remodel in a few years, a better solution is to keep permanent fixtures neutral and use towels, bath mats, tub decals, wall borders, and accessories like soap dispensers and toothbrush holders to add personality to the room. They're less expensive and much easier to replace.

small and half baths

Making the most of a smaller space

Small baths and half baths (powder rooms) represent different challenges than a master bath. The minimum size for a full bath containing a tub, toilet, and sink is 5 by 7 feet. The minimum size for a half bath with a sink and toilet is 3 by 6 feet. If you're working in an area that's roughly this size, it's best not to be too ambitious.

If you're modeling an existing bath that functions well as is, avoid fiddling with the placement of the fixtures. You could wind up with a beautiful, expensive new bathroom that doesn't function as well as the old one. Replace old fixtures with ones the same size or even smaller if you need to free up space.

If you need a bathing option here, install a slim, 32-square-inch shower unit. There are so many shower configurations available—even ones that can be squeezed under stairs or a low-hanging eave. If you can't live without a bathtub, try a tub/shower combo, a corner tub, or a soaking tub, which is deeper than a regular tub but doesn't take up as much floor space.

To visually expand a small bath, use light colors to decorate and make sure the room is properly lit. Mirrors will create the illusion of extra space, as will cabinets with mirrored doors. Avoid using partitions, which will make the space feel even more cramped. You can, however, raise the tub a few inches to define the space and create a sense of depth.

If you are renovating a powder room (a room with just a lavatory and toilet) remember that it doesn't have to work as hard as a full bath. Because no steam or moisture is generated from bathing, you can use wall and floor treatments that aren't as impervious to moisture. And the smaller surfaces mean you can use materials like marble that might be too expensive in a full bath. Plus, since lavatories and faucets are only used for hand washing, you can choose artistic fittings that might not be practical for family baths.

STORAGE SOLUTIONS

Storage is a crucial part of any bathroom plan, especially for a small bathroom. Consider the space you have to work with and what you need to store there. A powder room may require only spare rolls of toilet paper, soap, and guest towels, while a family bath may need much more storage.

Cabinets are usually your primary storage option and have a major impact on how your bathroom looks and functions. You can choose ready-to-assemble, stock, or custom-made cabinets in various materials and finishes (see pages 60–61), or a freestanding cabinet or bureau. If you have limited space, make use of the dead area high above the toilet by installing shelves, or purchase a floor-to-ceiling corner shelving unit.

The three other mainstays of bathroom storage are the vanity, the medicine cabinet, and the linen closet. There are two types of bathroom vanities. The most common is a vanity with a sink installed on top, which provides counter space around the sink and a cabinet underneath. You can also have a separate sink and vanity. In this case, the vanity features a flat surface on top and storage underneath. For small bathrooms, avoid buying a pedestal sink, which provides no storage options.

The typical medicine cabinet has a mirrored door and is placed over the sink, but many people are now opting for a larger mirror over the sink and a larger medicine cabinet in a separate location.

Linens are frequently stored in a closet or cabinet in the bathroom, but another option is to use a large linen closet in the hallway, which can also be used to store bed and/or table linens.

floors, walls, and surfaces

A guide to materials

A bathroom has many different surfaces: floor, ceiling, countertops, and walls. With all that water and moisture around, these surfaces have to be nonabsorbent and able to resist stains.

A bathroom also has surrounds. Just like the kitchen backsplash (see page 69), the bathroom surrounds are the wall areas that are directly exposed to water, usually behind the sink and around the tub. The shower also has a surround, usually the stall itself. These areas should be waterproof and consist of materials such as ceramic tile, solid surfacing material, stone, or glass brick.

When it comes to bathroom flooring, tile, vinyl (especially slip-resistant vinyl), laminate, and stone (often with radiant or electric heat installed underneath) are typical choices (see page 90).

When you go tile shopping, don't confuse floor tiles with wall tiles. Wall tiles aren't made to withstand floor use. You can use floor tiles on a wall, but they may be heavier than wall tiles, so make sure the adhesive you use is strong enough to hold them in place. Always discuss with your contractor or the tile supplier which adhesive to use for a particular tile.

While a bathroom countertop doesn't have to stand up to chopping and food stains, it does need to be moisture- and mildew-resistant and easy to clean.

Laminates, tile, and stone are popular choices for bathrooms. See page 66 for more on countertops.

Tip: You might consider installing extra insulation in the wall and a solid-core or solid wood door to muffle bathroom sounds.

Ask the Experts

What do I do if I love the look of a tile floor but hate the idea of scrubbing the grout or reapplying it?

A tile floor is indeed beautiful, but grout is not exactly easy to maintain. Simplify things by using silicone seal grout, which does a better job of holding up to wear and tear. Try gray or dark-colored grout, since white rarely stays pristine. You can also opt for a faux tile laminate floor. It will look like real ceramic tile but require no special upkeep.

What are my options if I use wallpaper in my bathroom and then later decide I don't like it?

The wallpaper industry is now making papers that can be removed from the wall without using water, ammonia, and scrapers, leaving the wall beneath undamaged. With peelable wallpaper, you simply peel the decorative outer layer off the wall, leaving behind the substrate, or liner, which can be used with new wallpaper. If you are unsure if you want to commit to wallpaper over the long term, choose strippable wallpaper. It can also be stripped from the wall, but leaves no secondary layer behind—just a minimal amount of paste or adhesive residue that can easily be cleaned off if you want to paint instead.

FIRST PERSON DISASTER STORY

Tile trauma

I installed beautiful bathroom wall tiles as a do-it-yourself job. I thought it would be simple, so I didn't bother to talk to an expert or read the instructions. A few months later, the tiles started cracking and pulling off the wall. I called a professional tile setter, who told me my wall's uneven surface was causing the problem. Apparently, tile must be laid on a completely smooth surface or underlayment (concrete board or moisture-resistant drywall). I'd also used an adhesive that was too weak. I ended up paying the tile setter to remove the tiles, smooth out the wall, and then reapply them. Never again will I try to do it myself without reading the directions first!

Alma R., Columbia, South Carolina

heating and ventilation

Keeping the bath warm and mildew-free

Nobody wants to step out of a hot bath or shower into a chilly bathroom. One economical option is to install a wall- or ceiling-mounted heater, which can warm up a small bathroom relatively quickly. If you are putting in a stone or tile floor, you can install a **radiant heat system** (if your home is heated by a boiler) under the floor, which uses hot water to warm up the floor, or an electric heating system underneath it.

If radiant or electric heat under the floor is not an option, try a toe-space or kick-space heater, which fits into the area between a base cabinet and the floor. They put out more heat than a typical baseboard heater and keep your feet and floor warm.

Wouldn't it also be nice to step out of the bath or shower and wrap yourself up in a warm, toasty towel? Go for a towel warmer—these units look like regular towel bars, racks, or shelves, but are heated by electricity or hot water.

Some people beat the chill by letting the bathroom steam up while bathing, but beware: Moisture can cause paint to peel and can sink into walls, damaging joists. Moisture also provides a breeding ground for that gruesome twosome of the bathroom, mold and mildew.

To stop mildew in its tracks, a window or an exhaust fan is key. Most building codes specify that a bathroom must include one or the other, but using both is even better. A recirculating fan moves air around but does not vent it out of the room, while a ducted system pulls moist air through ductwork and releases it outside. Ask your contractor which fan is best for your bath. You can even choose a wall- or ceiling-mounted fixture that combines a heating element, fan, and light in one unit.

You can also prevent mildew buildup by using mildew-resistant paint and purchasing fixtures made with Microban, an antibacterial additive applied during the manufacturing process.

Keeping yourself in hot water

If you are upgrading to a whirlpool tub or multiple showerheads, ask your contractor if your current water heater can handle the load or if you will need an additional one. A water heater dedicated to bathroom use will enable you to run the dishwasher or washing machine while showering or let people shower in different bathrooms at the same time without running out of hot water.

FINDING THE PERFECT FAN

When shopping for a bathroom fan, pay attention to its noise level and capacity.

Capacity: Fan capacity is rated in cubic feet per minute (cfm), which refers to the number of cubic feet of air a fan will move in one minute. To determine how many cfm your bathroom fan should have, measure the length, width, and height of your bathroom. Multiply these numbers to find the room's cubic footage, then divide this number by 7.5. The result is the number of cfm you need. Fans generally range from 70 to 600 cfm—although those over 200 are usually for commercial use.

Noise level: Fan noise is rated in sones. Don't worry, you don't have to do any more calculations! All you need to know is: The lower the sone, the quieter the fan. Bathroom fans typically range from one to four sones. The quietest set-up is an attic-mounted motor serving one or more intakes in the bathroom. For more information on fans and ventilation, go to the Heating and Ventilation Institute Web site at **www.hvi.org**.

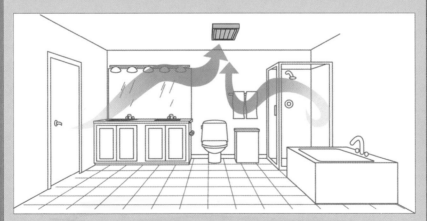

The proper exhaust fan can help reduce the high humidity levels common in bathrooms. High humidity is what causes mold and mildew to thrive, ruins paint, and destroys gypsum board.

tubs and whirlpools

An array of sizes, styles, and features

If you picture yourself relaxing in a sunken tub surrounded by flickering candles, you are not alone: A luxury tub is at the top of many bathroom wish lists. And no matter what your taste, there is a tub for you—from the old-fashioned, freestanding claw-foot type to feature-packed, ultramodern whirlpools (see opposite page).

Before you get carried away, first measure how much space you can allot to the tub. Consider who will be using the tub and how large they are. Will more than one person use the tub at once? Would you prefer a standard raised tub or a sunken unit?

Standard bathtubs are usually rectangular, but they can also be round or shaped like a pie slice to fit into corners. If you are really short on space, opt for a soaking, or sitting, tub (see page 86).

Bathtubs come in a range of materials. Acrylic is durable, lightweight, can be easily molded into various shapes, and helps bathwater retain heat. Fiberglass tubs are less expensive, but less resilient. Tubs can also be made of copper, cast iron, or marble. While these materials offer nostalgic charm, they are heavy to begin with and even more so when filled with water, so make sure your floor is strong enough to handle the weight.

Want to keep your current tub but make it look sparkling new again? Reglazing, in which the tub is sanded and a new glaze or enamel is applied, might be the perfect solution. You'll have to stay away from using harsh cleansers afterward, and even so, you will have to reglaze or replace the tub in about seven years. You can also restore an antique tub—but before you do, check with your plumber to see if it will work with modern plumbing and pipe sizes.

WHIRLPOOL TUBS

A whirlpool tub is something that many, many people dream of adding during a bathroom renovation. However, this is a major investment that needs to be researched carefully.

A whirlpool bath has jets that emit streams of bubbling, pulsating water to relax your muscles. When shopping for a whirlpool, make sure the jets are in the areas where you want massaging action, such as your back, neck, or feet. Some whirlpool baths have jets that draw in water and air for a more invigorating massage, while others use only air for a gentler, more relaxing sensation.

Before buying, it's a good idea to read the manual or ask the manufacturer, dealer, or your contractor exactly what upkeep is involved. You may need to disinfect the system's pipes about once a month using specified cleaners or have the jets checked or serviced on a regular basis. Some models have removable jets that can go right into the dishwasher.

showers

A relaxing soak in a tub may be an occasional pleasure, but a quick and invigorating shower is what gets most people through the day.

Like tubs, showers come in a vast array of styles. Standard shower enclosures are usually 32, 36, or 48 inches square and can be made of molded fiberglass, acrylic, solid surfacing material, ceramic tile, or stone. Some showers include foot whirlpools, steam units, benches, storage shelves, and even CD players.

If you can't find a prefabricated shower you like, you can always have one custom built. All it requires is a base with a hole for the drain, a surround (waterproof surface), and a door or partition.

You can even build a shower room instead of a full bath—this is basically a room you shower in. Because there's nothing else in the room, except perhaps a sink, you don't need a shower door or partition. The advantage of a shower room is that it can often fit into a small area that would not accommodate a full bath, and can alleviate bathroom congestion by separating the shower from the sink and toilet.

Aside from shower size and shape, consider the type of door you want. Pesky sliding doors are thankfully a thing of the past. Today's doors are made of clear or frosted glass and are usually hinged to open into the bathroom. If space is limited, choose a door that folds into the shower.

You can even add a bit of luxury with a personal steam room or sauna. Install a steam mechanism in your shower to produce humid heat, or build a sauna in a separate room. A sauna needs at least 50 square feet of space, a floor drain, and 220 volts of power. Adding a steam mechanism will cost about $1,000, while a sauna will start at about $4,000.

SHOWERHEADS

Showerheads run the gamut from the simple to the truly elaborate. And these days, even low-end models offer various settings so that you can go from a light spray to a pulsating massage. And many showerheads these days come with flow restrictors, which are often mandated by building and plumbing codes, or by local conservation regulations.

The most basic type is a fixed showerhead that attaches to the wall or ceiling. You can adjust the angle in order to aim the spray exactly where you want. A handheld showerhead is attached to the end of a short hose and can be placed in a wall-mounted socket or held while showering. Some have a slide bar with holders at different levels. This is a great solution if your family members are different heights.

If you are serious about your showers, move up from a single showerhead to a shower bar or even a floor-to-ceiling shower column. These units have several showerheads at different heights, providing massaging water action aimed at various parts of your body simultaneously. Or try a rainbar: a long metal bar hung horizontally or vertically on the wall or ceiling, which has numerous small openings and emits a gentle spray. A waterfall spout mimics a small waterfall, delivering a cascade of water.

If you have children or elderly people in your home, look for showerheads with thermostatic valves, which allow you to set the temperature and flow, or antiscald devices, which prevent the water from getting too hot.

toilets, sinks, and faucets

Admire the looks, but look for function

Walk into a sink and faucet showroom and you might think you were in a museum. These items can resemble Roman fountains or even avant-garde sculptures. Faucets alone range from the standard spout with "hot" and "cold" handles to artistic creations that barely resemble faucets at all. But don't be lured too much by looks—function is equally important. And beware that unusual design materials don't come cheap.

Bathroom sinks—often called lavatories—can be just as unusual; they are often made of ceramic, vitreous china, enameled steel, metal, glass, marble, or stainless steel.

One of the latest looks is the vessel sink: a freestanding basin mounted over the counter. While stunning to look at, these sinks are not very practical. You'll need to clean the sides and insides of the basin, as well as the countertop. This makes it a better choice for a powder room, where it won't be used, or need to be cleaned, as often.

If you really hate to clean, look for an integral sink, in which the sink and counter are a seamless unit. In a self-rimming or drop-in sink, the rim is over the countertop, and with an undermounted sink, it's slightly underneath. Because the rim is what gets gunked up, these styles are harder to clean than integral sinks.

Finally, you'll also need to choose the base. In a pedestal sink, the lavatory and base are one unit. While this style is great for small baths, it does not provide the counter and storage space of a vanity sink, which is a cabinet with a lavatory installed in the top.

When shopping for bathroom fixtures, try them out. No, you can't actually run the water in a showroom, but turn sink and tub handles to see how they work. Hop into a tub to see if it's comfortable. Most important, measure your bathroom doorway beforehand to make sure the items you want will fit through it.

TOILET TALK

Today's toilets come in a myriad of aesthetically pleasing designs, ranging from reproductions of their Edwardian forebears, complete with pull chains and wooden tanks, to futuristic units with a host of functions.

Toilets usually come in one-piece units, in which the tank and bowl are attached, or two-piece models, with a separate tank and bowl. They can be floor mounted or wall mounted—but only if your wall is strong enough to support the weight.

When it comes to water usage, federal law now mandates that all toilets sold use no more than 1.6 gallons of water per flush. Happily, today's low-flow toilets function much better than their predecessors, which often required a few flushes to do the job. But beware: Low-flow toilets may not work well with the plumbing in older homes, which have drainpipes designed for a greater flow rate.

Some toilets allow a choice between a 1.1-gallon flush or a 1.6-gallon flush with a flick of the lever. Others have extra-large, three-inch flush valves, which provide a more powerful flush; larger waste traps, which help prevent clogging; or pressure-assisted flushing action, which reduces loud noise.

In terms of new features, some toilets now have seats that warm up, mini water jets inside the bowl with adjustable temperature and pressure, or a small hose with a sprayer head, which works like a bidet. Bidets—low, toiletlike washbowls for cleaning your nether areas—are popular in Europe but are more of a novelty item in American bathrooms. They take up valuable bath space, so only install one if you really think you'll use it.

now what do I do?

Answers to common questions

I want to add a full bath, but I don't have a lot of room. How much space should there be between the toilet, tub, and sink?

Clearance, or the amount of space you need to leave around the major components of your bathroom, is the single most important element to good bathroom design. Gold-plated faucets won't be much comfort if you can't step out of your tub without bumping into a sink or toilet! Start by installing your tub or shower, leaving at least 30 inches in front. Next, put in the toilet, leaving 36 inches of foot room in front. Finally, position the sink, leaving at least 30 to 48 inches of clearance.

What are my options for bathroom wall areas that aren't surrounds?

Wall areas that don't get exposed to water can be painted, wallpapered, or even paneled. Choose washable vinyl wallpaper and mildew-resistant paint. A bathroom wall is also an excellent opportunity to try your hand at decorative painting (see page 115), since it's a relatively small surface area. Moldings and wainscoting (paneling that covers the lower half of the wall, see pages 112–113) add character to a traditional bath. Just make sure the wood is treated with urethane to protect it from moisture.

Can I retrofit my mother's old vanity table as a bathroom vanity with a sink?

You certainly can. Giving an old-fashioned mirrored vanity table or sideboard new life as a bathroom vanity is a popular way to add character to a bathroom. Just be sure it can support the weight of the sink you want to install, and treat the wood surface with a polyurethane finish to protect it against water and moisture. If this seems like too much work, you can purchase a bathroom vanity that resembles an antique dresser, perhaps with a weathered finish, but is manufactured to hold a sink. Vanity Flair (**www.vanityflair.com**) offers a wide selection. If the vanity you select doesn't have the timeworn finish you want, you can find books and magazines with instructions on how to "age" furniture yourself.

What are my options for enclosing a combination tub and shower unit?

The easiest and least expensive option is a shower curtain. These are available in a wide range of colors, patterns, and designs, and many can be matched with coordinating toothbrush holders, bath mats, towels, soap dispensers, and other accessories. When you're ready for a new look, simply buy a new set. One drawback to shower curtains is that they don't prevent splashes and leakage as well as other enclosures and can leave puddles on the floor if you're not careful. You can also enclose your tub/shower with a glass or plastic door, the same as you would a regular shower stall.

Should my bathroom's decor influence my lighting design?

Absolutely. Pale colors and shiny surfaces reflect light, while dark colors and textured surfaces absorb light. A bathroom with mahogany cabinets, a dark countertop, and a wood floor will need more lighting than a white room with a tile floor and mirrored cabinets.

Now where do I go?

BOOKS

The Smart Approach to Bath Design
by Susan Maney

Making the Most of Bathrooms
by Catherine Haig

DK Home Design Workbooks: Bathroom
by Suzanne Ardley

Ideas for Great Bathrooms
by the Editors of Sunset Books

WEB SITES

Kohler
www.kohler.com

The National Kitchen and Bath Association
www.nkba.org

The American Lighting Association
www.ala.org

Delta Faucet
www.delta.com

Jacuzzi
www.jacuzzi.com

Chapter 5

Living rooms

new looks for living rooms

Determine the room's purpose before remodeling

Before you dive into remodeling your living room, think about how the room will be used and by whom. If you have children, it could be time to turn that off-limits living room into a more casual space with durable flooring and walls. If your children are grown, you can transform a worn-out family room into an elegant space.

Is the room too dark? Additional lighting or an extra window might brighten things up. Is there enough storage? Put in shelving or add built-in units (see pages 184–185). If you're unhappy with the size or shape of the room, you can reorganize the space to better suit your needs. There are a range of possibilities:

Expand by building a bump-out or a separate addition as a new living room. Both entail excavating, laying a new foundation, construction, and heating and cooling the extra space, so first check your local zoning regulations regarding setbacks (see page 26).

Remove the walls between, say, a dining room and living room to create a large, open living/dining space. Open the rooms up to the kitchen as well to make one big great room. Just remember that if you remove a load-bearing wall you'll need to put in a header (see page 15).

Partition the space if you currently have a great room (see pages 120–121) and feel it's too open. Use contrasting floor and wall treatments to differentiate spaces, or raise the living room floor a few steps. Columns, arches, partitions, and walls also do the trick.

Raise the ceiling, taking advantage of unused attic space or an upstairs room. If you still need the extra room, create a loft: a small second-story area that overlooks the room below. A loft is a great place for a small home office or a reading area.

DECORATING STYLES

To create a coherent look for your living room—or any room, in fact—it helps if your furniture and the room's surfaces are similar in style. A decorating style can come from a particular time period, culture, or design school. Here's a look at the four most common design styles:

Traditional refers to pre-20th-century decorating styles, such as Baroque, French Provincial, Colonial, and Victorian. Dark wood finishes on floors and walls, marble floors or trim, wallpaper, crown moldings, and wainscoting (see pages 112–113), are all examples of Traditional elements. These rooms tend to be more formal.

Country also draws on the past, but is inspired by the furnishings of every-day folk, rather than the gentry, and is more casual than Traditional. Aside from America, Country styles come from England, France, Russia, Mexico, and many other nations and cultures. Weathered or painted wood, wooden-beamed ceilings, burled-wood or terra-cotta-tiled floors, wooden window shutters, and brick walls are typical elements.

Contemporary is based on styles developed after 1900 and includes Art Deco and Midcentury Modern. Contemporary rooms are usually less fussy and ornate than Traditional ones. Wall-to-wall carpeting; floors, furniture, and walls in light shades with no decorative details; track lighting; and steel-beamed ceilings are common touches for these casual rooms.

Eclectic homes mix furnishings and decor of different styles. To keep an Eclectic room from looking like a mishmash, unify it with a color or material.

Color and texture also help to create a formal or informal tone. Glossy surfaces, smooth textures, and dark or jewel-toned colors lend a more formal air, while matte surfaces, coarse or nubby textures, and light colors are more casual in feel.

a guide to windows

How to tell a bay from a bow

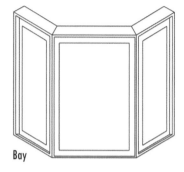

Bay

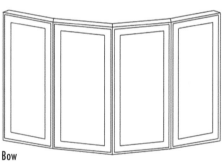

Bow

There's nothing like a window for brightening up a room. Windows let in sunlight and allow you to view the great outdoors from the comfort of indoors. The direction the window faces, or the exposure (see page 64), determines the amount of light and heat the room receives and affects the appearance of colors in the room.

Lots of windows once meant drafty rooms and higher energy bills. Not anymore. Today's windows are so energy efficient that you can add or enlarge window spaces where you please. Replacing your existing windows with more energy-efficient models can also help lower your fuel and utility bills.

Do you want to be able to open the window for ventilation? Fixed windows don't open and close; operable windows do. Here are some examples of each type.

Fixed windows

Bay A group of three or more windows set at angles to project outward, creating a bump-out where a window seat can be installed.

Bow Four or more adjoining windowpanes set at gentle angles to form a semicircle. This type does not project out as much as a bay.

Palladian An arched-top central window bordered by narrow rectangular windows on both sides.

Picture A large window that frames a pleasant exterior view.

Note: Bay and bow windows can also be operable.

Palladian

Operable windows

Awning A single pane, hinged at the top, that lifts up and out like an awning.

Casement A single pane, hinged at the side, that opens out.

Double hung A window with two panes that slide up and down; they can be opened from the top or bottom.

Sliding A two-paned window; one pane slides behind the other.

Hopper A small, narrow window often used at the top of basement walls. This can also be a fixed window.

Awning

DETERMINING A WINDOW'S ENERGY EFFICIENCY

A window's energy efficiency is rated in one of two ways:

R-value The R-value (also called R-factor) is the measure of the window's insulating capability. The more layers of glass, the higher the R-value. A single-pane window has an R-value of one; a double-pane window has a value of two; a window with argon gas sealed between the panes has an even higher value.

U-value Also called U-factor, U-value measures the amount of heat lost through the window. The U-value typically ranges from 0.20 to 1.20. The lower the U-value, the less heat is lost.

Applying a low-emissivity or (low-E) coating, which helps reflect heat, raises the R-value and lowers the U-value as well. Got it? You want a high R-value and a low U-value. For more information, contact the National Fenestration Rating Council (**www.nfrc.org**).

fireplaces

Remodeling or adding a hearth

There's just something about a roaring fire that warms the spirit and adds a spark of romance to your home. If you want to add or remodel a fireplace, your first decision is whether to go for a wood- or gas-burning one. A wood-burning fireplace offers the timeless appeal of crackling logs and the scent of wood smoke, while gas fireplaces offer the ambience of wood without the maintenance and cleanup hassles. There are two types of wood-burning fireplaces:

■ A masonry fireplace is constructed of brick and includes a firebox (the area that contains the fire) and a chimney. You will have to reinforce the floor and improve the foundation beneath the fireplace, and possibly put in special supports to bear the weight.

■ A prefabricated fireplace is built mostly out of metal. Because it is more lightweight, you won't need to do any foundation work. This unit includes the firebox and chimney, and is easier to install and less expensive than a masonry fireplace.

Gas units come in both masonry and metal styles and have permanent ceramic logs that emit gas flames. In some units the logs are fixed in place; in others, you can arrange them. If you choose a gas fireplace, install a carbon monoxide detector that will sound an alarm if the levels of this potentially fatal gas get too high.

Unless your locality restricts it, you can also choose between a direct-vent gas fireplace, which releases gases outside via ductwork, and a vent-free unit, which has burners that reduce carbon monoxide, so it does not require venting.

Also consider the placement of your fireplace and chimney. A fireplace built into an exterior wall will take up less floor space than one installed in an interior wall. However, the latter can be viewed from either side and thus enjoyed from two rooms.

Ask the Experts

I can't decide which kind of fireplace to install. What are the pros and cons of wood versus gas?

With a gas fireplace, you don't have to gather firewood, clean out the ashes, or worry about the buildup of creosote, a wood-smoke residue that is highly flammable. You can even switch units on or off and adjust the height of the flames via remote control. As nifty as these features may be, for some people they just don't substitute for the romance of a wood-burning fireplace. Your decision may come down to what type of system is permitted in your area. Some localities restrict the use of wood fireplaces; others don't allow vent-free gas units.

I'm thinking about putting in a wood-burning fireplace. What kind of maintenance will it require?

You'll need to have your fireplace and chimney inspected about once a year, depending on how frequently you use it, to make sure there's no creosote buildup. A professional chimney sweeper can save you the hassle of climbing on your roof. To learn more, contact the Chimney Safety Institute of America (**www.csia.org**).

I like the antique look of coal- and wood-burning stoves. Are these reasonable alternatives to a fireplace?

Yes, and in fact, these can be much more fuel efficient than a gas or wood-burning fireplace. In the past, wood-burning stoves were linked with respiratory ailments and environmental problems, but today's newer models are much improved. (Be wary of buying antiques for this reason.) If you decide on a coal-burning stove, then be sure to use anthracite coal, which burns cleaner than other kinds of coal.

Stayin' alive

Two of the most serious home safety hazards are fires and CO_2 (carbon monoxide), a poisonous gas emitted by furnaces, fireplaces, and gas water heaters and dryers. Install smoke and CO_2 detectors on every level of your home and check the batteries often. If you have an electric model, make sure it has a backup battery in case of a power outage.

lighting to live with

Lighting is about so much more than just illuminating a dark room. As any photographer or lighting director will tell you, lighting creates a mood. Think of the difference between a bright, shadowless home office and a candlelit dining room where you enjoy a romantic dinner.

Before you renovate your living room, discuss with your builder the wiring, number, and placement of outlets (all regulated by code), so you can plan the best locations for your furniture, lamps, and light fixtures. Spotlights, track lights, and wall sconces are installed directly into the electrical connection in the wall or ceiling. You can replace the fixtures themselves if need be, but if the electrical wiring and connection aren't there, you'll have to open up the walls to add them later. And although you can use extension cords to plug floor and table lamps into wall outlets, you'll probably appreciate having outlets installed near your lamps.

Artificial lighting falls into three categories.

Ambient light provides the primary lighting for your room. The usual source is an overhead fixture. Put it on a dimmer switch to adjust it according to the mood or activity.

Task lighting is used for a particular task. A desk lamp or a track light over a piano are typical examples.

Accent lighting draws attention to an element you wish to highlight, such as artwork.

Lighting fixtures and lamps may replicate antique styles or be strikingly innovative and modern. Formal chandeliers, tall Victorian floor lamps, resplendent Tiffany table lamps, and Modern paper lamps—you're sure to find something that suits your style.

The appearance of a beam of light is also affected by the type of bulb you use. Bulbs affect your electric bills as well, since some are more energy efficient than others (see page 109).

Bright idea

If you're rewiring your living room, consider having some outlets wired so that the bottom plug is always active (for a TV, stereo, etc.) and the top one is controlled via a switch plate on the wall. This way, you can easily turn on a table lamp when entering a dark room.

A Incandescent bulb
B Halogen bulb
C Fluorescent bulb

THE RIGHT BULB FOR THE JOB

Your lighting needs can most likely be served by either incandescent, fluorescent, or halogen bulbs. Here's how they compare:

Incandescent bulbs emit a light that's even warmer in tone than sunlight and thus flattering to most skin shades. They are a good choice for bedrooms and areas where you entertain, such as the living room. The downside: They are the least energy efficient bulbs.

Halogen bulbs produce a brighter and hotter light that's whiter in tone. They're about twice as energy efficient as incandescents, but more expensive. Because the light they emit is more focused, they are best for task or accent lighting, rather than general lighting.

Fluorescent bulbs are the most energy efficient. Newer versions have done away with the unflattering glare and are quieter and much warmer in tone. There are two types of fluorescent bulbs, tubular and compact, which come in standard bulb sizes.

FIRST PERSON DISASTER STORY
In the dark

We carefully planned our living room renovation to the last detail, but didn't think much about lighting beyond including one overhead light and outlets for floor and table lamps. I wish we'd paid more attention to lighting design and had worked track lighting and wall sconces into the plan. They would have dispersed the light better, freed up floor and table space, and done away with all those wires running behind tables and sofas.

Kyoshi H., Milpitas, California

wiring for home theater and more

Audio, video, networking, and automation

Once upon a time, your home entertainment needs were met by a TV and a stereo. Then along came the VCR, the DVD player, computers, and video games, not to mention high-speed Internet connections, high-definition television, and advanced home security systems. Who knows what the future will bring?

Regular phone and video lines simply don't offer enough speed and capacity for high-tech systems. So if your renovation involves opening up the walls, consider upgrading your wiring. You'll need Category 6—or at least Category 5— twisted-pair wire to carry voice and high-speed data transmissions and RG6 quad shield coaxial cable for the high-definition video provided by some cable and satellite TV companies.

While you're at it, consider networking your home so all your home computers can share data, printers, and an Internet or broadband connection. You will also be able to download music on your computer and play it on your stereo in another room.

If you're a true technophile, you may want to look into home automation and also install a high-tech security system. An automated home has touch pads in various locations for accessing video, audio, lighting, heating, air conditioning, and your home security system. You can install a touch pad, speaker, and flat screen TV next to your bathtub, bed, or kitchen sink. Then, with a few taps on the panel, you can play a CD, change the TV channel, or check out who's at the front door via your security camera.

Not sure what you want in terms of high-tech equipment? Install conduits (hollow plastic tubes) in the walls now to make rewiring easier when you're ready for it. At the very least, choose where to hang or place your stereo speakers and enclose the wiring to avoid unsightly wires running along or hanging from walls. You can house your TV and other components and accessories in a built-in unit or freestanding armoire.

Ask the Experts

Why should I install high-tech wiring when I can use a wireless network?

Though you may have a cellular phone, chances are you still rely on a landline, too, because of its consistent quality. Like cell phones, wireless fidelity, or wi-fi, products and networks send and receive data wirelessly; they are likewise subject to interference from competing signals and vulnerable to intruders. Plus, they don't yet offer the data transmission speed of wired networks. Wi-fi is okay if you aren't renovating, but if you know you want a home network and are opening up the walls anyway, save yourself the headache and install a wired network now. You can always add wireless components to your wired network later on.

I'm interested in installing a home security system when I upgrade my wiring. Where do I begin?

A home security system can be a relatively simple affair or a complex, high-tech setup like something out of a spy film. Obviously, the more elaborate the system, the pricier it is. The good news is that many insurance companies will reduce your premium if you install one. If you're renovating or rewiring your home, this is a great time to put in a wired security system, since some alarm systems interface with a phone line. (You can also opt for a system that combines wired and wireless.) Always hire a professional to do the job. The National Burglar and Fire Alarm Association, **www.alarm.org**, offers advice for consumers and posts a list of qualified professionals.

architectural details

Adding character with moldings, trim, and wainscoting

When renovating your living room, think about how you can give the room a distinctive look with architectural details—the fixed, built-in elements that give your home its style.

For example, you can install moldings. These decorative window and wall edgings were traditionally made of wood or plaster, but nowadays you can also buy easy-to-install foam moldings that can be finished to look like painted wood; they sometimes feature carved leaves, vines, and other details.

When molding is used to trim doors, windows, or cabinets it's called casing. If it's installed where the floor and wall meet, it's called a baseboard. Molding between a wall and ceiling is sometimes called a cornice. Living room ceilings can also be detailed with wooden beams or plaster rosettes (see page 122).

Another popular architectural detail is the chair rail: a long, thin strip of wood, foam, or plaster that traverses the wall at chair height, about a third of the way up. Chair rails are practical as well as aesthetically pleasing. That's because the lower half of the wall, called the dado, is what usually receives bumps and knocks from chairs and feet, so you can use a more durable or less expensive wall covering underneath the rail and a pricier treatment in the safer space above it.

Traditionally, the dado is covered with wainscoting. This usually refers to wood paneling, but it also includes any wall covering used on the lower third of a wall.

Picture rails are similar to chair rails, but are placed at about eye level. The name comes from the fact that they provide a place to install hooks for hanging artwork.

One thing to note: Rails, baseboards, and mantels can be dust collectors. While the dust isn't excessive, you may want to avoid these details if you have allergies.

Ask the Experts

Our Modern ranch house has ornate moldings and baseboards installed by the previous owner. Our designer says these clash with the house's style, as well as with our Contemporary furniture. Is he right?

Yes. Moldings, chair rails, and wainscoting are Traditional elements that have been with us for centuries and go with many period styles. Highly decorative moldings don't work as well with Modern or Contemporary decor styles, which are not as fussy and feature more sparse, unadorned surfaces. However, if you're going for a more eclectic look in your living room, feel free to experiment and use whatever pleases you.

What are my options when it comes to choosing a shape and style for my moldings?

The sky is really the limit when it comes to molding designs. They are available in a wide range of styles, most of which are inspired by different time periods, such as the Georgian or Victorian eras. Some popular styles include crown moldings, which curve outward and often have raised details carved into them, and cove moldings, which curve inward, softening the sharp angle between the wall and ceiling. Dental, or dentil, moldings have raised squares or rectangles that resemble teeth (hence the name).

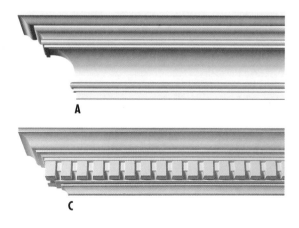

A Cove molding
B Crown molding
C Dental molding

wall treatments

Paint, wallpaper, and paneling

When it comes to picking a wall treatment as part of your renovation project, your choices are nearly limitless.

Paint is the least expensive choice. Gloss and semigloss paints have a shiny appearance, while a flat finish is more matte. There are also finishes in between, like eggshell and satin. You can choose from a myriad of colors or even bring a fabric swatch or carpet sample to a paint dealer and have him customize a shade to match your sofa, carpet, or window treatments.

The beauty of wallpaper is that you won't need to repaint. It's priced by the roll, but usually packaged by the continuous double or triple roll. A pattern number and dye-lot or run number, which designates the roll's print run, is stamped on each roll. Since color, coating, and embossing can vary according to the dye lot or run, it's a good idea to order extra wallpaper for your job and record the pattern and dye-lot numbers in case you need to order more rolls.

Paneling is available in two types. Solid wood paneling is composed of hardwood planks. Solid wood is elegant, but more expensive than sheet paneling, which consists of wood veneers bonded to plywood. Sheet paneling may also be a laminate that resembles wood. You may remember sheet paneling as a cheap-looking covering relegated to basements and dens, but today's sheet paneling is made with higher-quality materials and finishes and is often an improvement over what was available 10 or 20 years ago.

Can't decide what to do? Be creative. You can wallpaper one wall or paint it a different color from the other walls, use a contrasting paint color for windowsills, moldings, and trim, or apply paneling on the bottom half of a wall and paint the top half.

Ask the Experts

How can I be sure that the paint color I choose will look right in my living room?

Before you paint an entire wall, paint small squares or tape paint chips on the wall. Observe the colors in natural light throughout the course of the day and then at night under artificial lighting. Paler hues and cool colors tend to tone down the warm, intense light from a southern exposure. If your windows face north, choose warm colors to brighten up the pale, bluish cast of northern light.

My neighbor has the most beautiful sponge-painted walls in her living room. Is this technique hard to master?

Most decorative painting techniques are fairly easy to do, even if crafts have never been your strong point. With minimal effort, you can even learn to mimic the look of marble, terra-cotta, or plaster. Usually, you apply a base coat and then use another color or glaze to create the effect. Ragging will give your walls the look of distressed leather, while dragging creates a woven-fabric effect. In sponging, you apply dabs of paint using—you got it—a sponge.

GET THE LEAD OUT

Usually found in lead-based paint or lead-soldered pipes, lead is a contaminant to watch out for in older homes. This should either be encapsulated or removed by a qualified professional.

Solving room problems with wall coverings

Ceiling too low Use a wall covering with vertical stripes or an open design. Leave the ceiling white.

Ceiling too high Use warm, dark colors and a covering with an all-over pattern, such as paisley.

Strangely shaped room Use a wall covering with a soft background or an all-over pattern to mask architectural oddities.

Architecturally boring room Use various features to create interest, like a chair rail or wainscoting, and wallpaper borders at the ceiling.

Room too small Use a wall covering with a loosely spaced pattern to give the walls depth.

Room too big Use a wall covering with a large pattern to make the room cozier.

No view Create one with a large mural or mosaic. Your options are limitless, from an Asian-inspired scene to an Italian fresco.

now what do I do?

Answers to common questions

Should I use oil or latex paint on my living room walls?

Oil paint has lost ground to water-based latex paint over the years because it emits harmful fumes, but it is still used sometimes in kitchens, bathrooms, and playrooms because it is durable. Latex paint is safer to breathe and adequate for most uses. If you'll be doing the painting yourself, use latex. Working with oil paint is best left to a professional. You'll still have to provide plenty of ventilation and vacate your home or close off the room until the paint has dried.

I have a great room with a fireplace. How can I make the area around the fireplace cozier?

Create an alcove around the fireplace using partial walls or partitions. Be sure to include space inside the area for seating. By the way, a fireplace area that is separated slightly from the rest of the room is called an inglenook. Isn't it practically worth creating one just so you can use this charming term?

I'm looking at a surround-sound home entertainment system. Where do all these different speakers go?

If you're like most people, you've put a seating area directly in front of your TV to maximize the effect. If this is the case, place the center channel speaker, which is primarily for dialogue, on top of the TV, or mount it above. An additional speaker goes on each side, about a foot away from the TV. For theater-quality sound, put two more speakers on the other side of the room, to the right and left of the seating area. Depending on the size of your room, you can mount these speakers on the rear or side walls, about six feet high. Place a low-frequency subwoofer for deep bass sounds anywhere in the room, except in a corner. Your best bet is to have these speakers installed by a professional. If you choose to do it yourself, read the manufacturer's manual carefully.

Do I have to get a building permit to add or change a window?

It depends on where you live, so check with the building department in your city. Adding or enlarging a window could compromise your home's structure, so it usually requires a permit and a visit from your local inspector. Replacing a window with one the same size rarely requires a permit. Keep in mind that if you live in a historic district, you may be limited in terms of what exterior changes you can make to your home.

My designer says we need to choose a focal point for the living room before remodeling. What is this and why do I need one?

The focal point is the first thing you notice when you walk into a room. It can be an architectural element, such as a fireplace or a bay window, or a movable element, such as a wide-screen TV, colorful chaise, painting, or piano. Depending on the size of your room, you could have from one to four focal points in different areas. If your living room is fairly nondescript and you have the budget, adding an architectural element can turn your living room into a showstopper. If you choose instead to use a movable element as a focal point, deciding where to place it beforehand will determine which walls will play center stage and where you will put outlets and lighting fixtures. This will help you avoid problems like covering up a decorative wall or not lighting the focal point properly.

Now where do I go?

BOOKS

Chris Casson Madden's New American Living Rooms
by Chris Casson Madden with Carolyn Schultz

The Home Decorator's Bible
by Anoop Parikh, Debora Robertson, Thomas Lane, Elizabeth Hilliard, and Melanie Paine

Better Homes and Gardens: Fireplaces: Decorating and Planning Ideas

Making the Most of Living Rooms
by Amanda Evans

WEB SITES

Electronic House magazine
(**www.electronichouse.com**)

The Wallcoverings Association
(**www.wallcoverings.org**)

The International Association of Lighting Designers
(**www.iald.org**)

The National Paint and Coatings Association Information Center
(**www.paintinfo.org**)

The Hearth Products Association
(**www.hearthassoc.org**)

The Hearth Education Foundation
(**www.hearthed.com**)

Chapter 6

Dining rooms

6

dining rooms vs. great rooms

One large room vs. separate living and dining rooms

A few years ago, some design pundits were predicting that dining rooms would be replaced by dining areas in the kitchen, living room, or family room. As predicted, it is now a big trend to join the dining room to the kitchen or living room, creating a great room.

This is a popular choice because a great room opens up your living space. And it makes sense if you like casual dining or don't entertain formally very often. You can eat while you watch TV, keep an eye on your children, or talk to whoever is cooking in the kitchen.

But there are still those who prefer to have a separate dining room. Nothing can replace the timeless pleasure of getting out your best china, creating a centerpiece, and treating your guests or family members to an elegant meal in a room devoted to their enjoyment.

Separate dining rooms have other benefits as well. Some of us like having a more formal room that's off-limits to children and pets. Plus, while the decor of a dining area in a great room usually matches the living room and kitchen, you can use more formal fittings and furnishings in a separate dining room to create a theatrical mood. Murals on the walls or ceiling will offer a dramatic backdrop to meals, and a chandelier can be an unusual conversation piece.

Of course, there's no reason why you have to have a fancy, "off-limits" dining room if you have young children. You can make the dining room the heart of your home by outfitting it in durable materials and using it for everyday meals, as well as special occasions.

Because it is a separate room, the dedicated dining room is relatively easy to remodel. But before deciding on wall and floor treatments, you should choose a decor style (see page 103). Take a cue from your dining set. Is it Traditional? A dark, shiny hardwood floor, wainscoting, and moldings will work well. Try sleekly painted walls with no trim to go with a Modern dining set, and a faux-aged finish on walls for a homey look to complement a Country-style table and chairs.

Ask the Experts

I want to turn my unused study into a dining room, but I'm afraid it's too small. How much space do I need?

The size you need depends on how many people you want to seat. For example, if you plan to seat 10 to 12 people, you'll need a room at least 13 feet square. You also need to think about clearance (the amount of space to leave around furnishings). Leave at least 32 inches from the edge of the table to the wall for people to pull out a chair and sit down, or 38 inches from edge of table to wall for someone to walk behind a seated diner. Increase that to 42 inches to accommodate someone carrying trays or platters. If you're short on space, instead of chairs you can place one side of the table in front of a built-in bench, or banquette (see page 56).

I have a great room and I want to separate the dining area a little more from the kitchen and living areas. What are my options?

The trouble with great rooms is they can sometimes be too open. You don't have to resort to putting up walls, however. Use contrasting flooring and wall treatments or area rugs to differentiate spaces. Partially separate areas by installing columns, arches, or partitions. Sliding pocket doors or Japanese shoji screens, which are sliding screen doors covered with translucent paper, can be left open or closed to either open up the dining room or separate it from the rest of the space. You can also raise the living room a few steps, but this isn't advisable for the dining room. No one wants to trip while they're carrying hot foods or china back and forth between the kitchen and dining room!

ceilings

Height, color, and
decorative elements

Often the ceiling is simply painted every few years and then pretty much forgotten about, but a ceiling with a few special touches can have a dramatic impact on a dining room.

If you have a seldom-used room or unused attic space overhead, consider raising the ceiling, which can make the room feel much

grander. But beware that raising a ceiling can be tricky—and expensive. If there's no upper story, it can mean removing the roof and building a new one. Plus, you'll pay more to heat and cool that extra space overhead.

Removing the original ceiling may leave you with a vaulted ceiling with exposed rafters. Another option is creating a high, domed ceiling illuminated by lights hidden above a wall molding (see pages 112–113), or raising just the center of the ceiling and installing a tesselated wooden frame fitted with large, flat light panels. A ceiling fan hung in the center often completes this look. A coffered ceiling is another possibility, in which the ceiling is raised and then crisscrossing soffits, or long narrow beams, are set in a gridlike pattern.

If raising the ceiling isn't in the cards, put in ceiling beams to add character, or add a formal ceiling rosette or medallion, a raised decorative design that usually surrounds a chandelier. They have traditionally been made of plaster, but these days you can buy one made of hard plastic, which you simply glue to the ceiling. For a more contemporary look, try mirroring the ceiling. A skylight (see page 155) is another way to add interest and let in light.

An easier, cheaper way to make a ceiling appear higher is to paint it a lighter color than the walls. If your ceiling is too high, painting it a darker color will make it appear lower. If you're feeling creative, paint a simple mural, or add texture with a decorative faux finish.

Ask the Experts

I'm restoring a Victorian house. Any ideas for a period ceiling treatment?

Try a tin ceiling. These ornately patterned panels were popular in the 19th century and are experiencing a resurgence. The panels are available in a range of finishes and are relatively easy to install. Check out Brian Greer's tin ceilings at **www.tinceiling.com**.

If I remove my existing dining room ceiling to create a vaulted one, what are my options for overhead lighting?

If you prefer to have a center fixture, rather than perimeter lighting hidden by a ledge or wall molding, a good bet is to purchase a ceiling fan/light with an extension downrod (a long pole that runs from the ceiling to the fixture). This way, the light will hang lower and illuminate the room rather than the ceiling. If the ceiling is steeply sloped, look for a unit with a canopy (the enclosure which attaches to the ceiling and houses the electrical box) that is designed to accommodate such ceilings. Another possibility is to install horizontal ceiling beams and attach lighting fixtures, such as track lighting, to these rather than to the ceiling itself.

FIRST PERSON DISASTER STORY

Burning Up

My partner and I decided to use the attic space over our dining room to create a 16-foot ceiling and we were really happy with the result. That is, until we started to notice that the room now felt much colder in the winter and hotter in the summer. We finally got tired of cranking up the heat and air conditioning and called an architect for advice. He told us that breaking into the attic meant that in winter the heat was now rising to the top of that very high ceiling, and in summer it was accumulating in the room, rather than in the attic. The solution was to add a ceiling fan to circulate the air around and out of the room. I wish we'd researched this before we got socked with all those sky-high electric bills!

Jack M., Old Orchard Beach, Maine

lighting, storage, and display

Your dining room can be an excellent showroom for everything from your table and dinnerware to artwork, china, and collectibles. Even if your dining room is casual, you're sure to have some items or elements of the room that you want to highlight.

A common choice is an eye-catching light fixture over the table. Not only does this fixture provide light to dine by, it also acts as a sort of centerpiece. An elegant chandelier is a typical option, but lighting fixtures can certainly be a lot more unusual. Put the light on a dimmer switch so you can change the mood from upbeat, for children's birthday parties, to subtle, for romantic dinners.

Accent lighting, used to highlight a decorative object, can really be put to work in a dining room. Use it to spotlight artwork on the walls. Does the room have a china or curio cabinet? Attach low-voltage strips of minilights under the shelves to illuminate collections. Run the wiring through a small hole drilled in the back of the cabinet. You can also buy a cabinet with a false back, so that the hole will be in the actual back of the cabinet, invisible from view.

If your dinnerware and glassware are worthy of display, install shelving to show them off. The shelves will also act as open storage, keeping these items handy for serving. You may also want to add cabinets or drawers for items you don't choose to put on view. A sideboard—a long, low cabinet with drawers—is particularly useful for this. The surface is convenient for platters, trays, or extra plates, and the drawers underneath offer concealed storage for items like flatware and linens.

Ask the Experts

How high above the table should I hang my chandelier?

A chandelier should be about 30 inches above the tabletop. So before you install it, you'll need to know the height of your ceiling in order to ensure that your fixture won't be too high or too low. Some chandeliers have extension rods so you can adjust the height.

My renovated dining room is going to be a multipurpose room. What kind of task lighting do I need?

That depends on what you'll be doing in there. If you'll be carving turkeys or doing any food prep from a sideboard, you may want to include lighting over that area. If you'll use your dining room table during the week for paperwork or hobbies, you could install track lighting or spotlights over one side for additional lighting. Look at what other activities you plan to do in the room. Do you want to read from a window seat or chair? Will the room double as a guest room or home office? You'll want to include appropriate task lighting for these functions as well.

I rarely get to sit down and enjoy a meal with my guests because I'm always running to and from the kitchen with dishes that need to be kept warm. Is there a solution?

You've put your finger on a dilemma that baffles many hosts. Here's an idea: Purchase a sideboard along with some electric burners or hot plates. Find a good location in the room for the sideboard, and install electrical wiring and outlets in the wall next to or behind it. This way, dishes and platters can be kept warm right in your dining room rather than in the kitchen, which will save you from running around.

double-duty dining rooms

When it's a library, home office, or activity area

Odds are you don't use your dining room much, unless you entertain frequently. But this doesn't mean it should collect dust. Think about other ways you can use the dining room and renovate accordingly.

Is your dining room the best spot for doing homework or playing board games? Would you like to use it as an art studio or a hobby room? Include storage units or additional work surfaces.

Is your kitchen table buried under mail, newspapers, and paperwork? Use the dining room for this instead, especially if you don't use it frequently. A filing cabinet or built-in shelving unit (see page 184) can help here.

If you've always wanted a library but don't have the extra room, let your dining room double as one. If you have some extra space here, you can create a reading area that's much more private and quiet than what you'd have in a living or family room. A window seat or chair, an end table, and good lighting will make a cozy reading nook. And a wall of bookshelves is an attractive backdrop to a sit-down dinner.

Need a place to put your home office? If your dining set doesn't take up too much space, you may be able to put a small computer desk in a corner or against a wall. Use a screen or curtain to conceal your home office when you are using the room for dining.

Ask the Experts

Can I use my dining room as a guest room?

You certainly can. The trick is to use furniture that folds. Purchase a dining table with removable leaves and folding chairs. Set a sofa bed or fold-up futon couch against the wall. When guests need the room, fold up the table and chairs and unfold the bed. Make sure that the room has a door or at least a curtain or folding screen to give guests some privacy, and that it's located near a bathroom. If your dining room isn't carpeted, you could also arrange small area rugs near the bed so guests don't have to step on a cold floor in the morning.

We use our dining room for everything from studying to sewing. What kind of decor is best for this kind of multipurpose room?

It's best not to have a room that shouts "dining room." Stay away from plate racks and curio displays in favor of a more neutral approach, with fairly nondescript walls, floor, and window treatments. Take your cue from the other functions the room will serve. If young children will be using it or you want to use the room for scrapbooking or hobbies, choose flooring that's easy to clean. If the room will also be a guest room, you may want to paint the walls a soft, soothing color, rather than using red or a busy wallpaper pattern, and put in carpeting or a rug.

Decorating tip

Having a multipurpose dining room doesn't mean you have to forgo an elegant dining table and chairs. You can cover them with a tablecloth and slipcovers when not in use. On the flip side, even the plainest, least expensive tables and chairs can be dressed up with textiles, which can be put away when it's time to get some office work done.

now what do I do?

Answers to common questions

We are remodeling our home and the designer thinks we should add a butler's pantry next to the dining room. What is this for?

A butler's pantry is a small annex between the kitchen and dining room that is used to store supplies like tableware and linens. It can act as a buffer zone between the two rooms if you don't always want to leave your kitchen open to guests. Before you include a butler's pantry in your plans, make sure you can give up the extra space and that you'll put this small room to good use.

Is it better to build my new deck off the dining room or living room?

Do you plan on using the deck mostly for outdoor dining? If so, locating it directly outside the kitchen/dining room area will make carting out food, linens, glasses, dinnerware, and other supplies that much easier. Plus, you and your guests can quickly relocate to the dining room if the weather suddenly turns nasty. Install glass doors off your dining room for easy access and to create the effect of one large indoor/outdoor room.

Can I include a fireplace in my dining room?

You certainly can. After all, there's nothing like a holiday dinner in front of a roaring fire. Even when there's no fire in the grate, a fireplace and mantel (see page 106) can add a lot of decorative interest to your dining room. But adding a fireplace can be quite an undertaking. Be sure to discuss your wishes with an architect and find out if there are any building codes in your area that restrict the use of wood-burning fireplaces or vent-free gas units (see page 106).

What are some good colors for my dining room walls?

Color influences our moods and energy levels. You'll notice that restaurants often use red, yellow, or orange decor to stimulate diners' appetites, so go with these colors to liven up dinners. If you want your dining room to be more soothing, opt for cool colors. You can't go wrong heeding the old adage "blue and white is always right." This color combination works well in any room but can be particularly effective in your dining room, especially if you use blue and white china.

My dining room is tiny and has no windows. How can I make it appear more spacious?

Use color and pattern. Dark tones and warm hues like red, yellow, and orange make rooms seem smaller. Cool colors like blue and green, as well as pastels, make walls appear to recede. If you prefer wallpaper, use a small pattern with a lot of space between the pattern designs to lend a more open feeling, or vertical stripes that will make the walls seem taller. You can also use a large mirror to create the illusion of space.

Can my dining room double as a playroom?

It can, but it will take a little compromise on your part. Forgo a formal dining room in favor of a casual dining space. Use a laminate or vinyl floor that looks like wood, tile, or stone instead of the real thing, and provide hidden storage space for toys in the form of built-in shelving units (see page 184) or a closet. Get the playful function of the room to work for you, perhaps by hanging your children's artwork or photos in lieu of paintings. If this all sounds like a bit much to you, and you hardly use the dining room anyway, then just turn the room into a dedicated playroom until the children are older.

Now where do I go?

BOOKS

The House and Garden Book of Kitchens and Dining Rooms
by Leonie Highton

Colors for Your Every Mood
by Leatrice Eiseman

**Creative Home Design:
Rooms for Everyday Living**
By Lisa Skolnik, Rima A. Sugi,
and Barbara Ballenger Buchholz

WEB SITES

The American Lighting Association
www.ala.org

The National Paint and Coatings Association Information Center
www.paintinfo.org

The Wallcoverings Association
www.wallcoverings.org

The American Society of Interior Designers
www.asid.org

Chapter 7

Bedrooms

master bedrooms

They're getting larger and more elaborate

If you are like most people, you probably feel overwhelmed at times by the demands of your busy life. So it's no wonder that many people are choosing to turn their master bedrooms into luxurious, spa-like suites for relaxing and recouping. Perhaps taking a cue from hotel rooms, some homeowners have even turned their bedrooms into deluxe private retreats—almost mini-apartments—complete with sitting areas, refrigerators, and wet bars. Or their bedrooms also serve as exercise rooms or home offices.

What do you want in your master bedroom? Standard amenities include a queen- or king-size bed, a desk, an armchair or two or a window seat for a small sitting area, ample closet space, and perhaps a vanity or dressing table. Do you like to watch TV from bed? Plan where you'll house your home entertainment system, and extend your high-speed wiring to your bedroom (see page 110).

What size bed do you want? A 78- by 80-inch king-size bed is more luxurious than a 60- by 80-inch queen, but think about whether you could use that extra space for a dresser, chair, or other furniture. If you're renovating a solo retreat, you may want to give yourself even more room by using a 54- by 75-inch full-size bed.

If your bedroom is on the ground floor, you can include a door that opens onto your deck, patio, or yard. For an upstairs bedroom, add a balcony or roof garden. Either way, you extend your comfort and relaxation to the outdoors.

CREATING A BETTER BEDROOM

How do you create the master bedroom of your dreams? You have many options when it comes to reorganizing space in your house:

Steal space If your existing bedroom is too small, your easiest option is to expand it by taking space from another room, perhaps an adjoining bedroom or hall closet. Adding a small bay-window bump-out (see page 15) can give you enough space for a window seat. Plus, you'll get extra light and extra storage under the seat.

Add a second story If you can't steal space from anywhere else to create your ideal master suite and you live in a one-story house, consider adding a second story. First, however, you'll need to consult an architect or structural engineer to see whether your house's structure and foundation can handle the weight of an upper floor. Since you'll be tearing out your existing roof, try to schedule your renovation for the warmer, drier months.

Add another room Perhaps you would prefer to build a ground-floor addition instead of a second story. If so, keep in mind that this is usually more expensive and takes longer to build. You'll have to excavate and lay a foundation, and if the new addition extends your house toward the road, you'll need to check with your building department about frontage regulations (frontage is the distance required between the road and your house). On the other hand, a more accessible ground-floor master bedroom might make a lot of sense, particularly if you plan on retiring in your home.

Reassign room responsibilities Perhaps you can get away with not making any structural changes by simply reassigning room responsibilities. Perhaps there's a living room, playroom, or family room you don't need anymore. Add walls and a door, and you've got a bigger, brand-new bedroom. You can even kill two birds with one stone by turning your old bedroom into a guest room.

carpets and area rugs

Looking at soft floor coverings

Carpets and rugs are a natural fit for bedrooms. Who wouldn't prefer to sink their bare toes into a plush carpet rather than be greeted by a cold floor first thing in the morning? Soft floor coverings also offer some soundproofing, which can help keep your teenager's music from penetrating to your living room below.

Choose your carpet: above, area rug. Opposite page, **A** loop pile, **B** cut pile, **C** cut and loop pile.

People often use the terms *carpet* and *rug* interchangeably, but there is a difference. Area rugs come in various sizes and are laid over a finished floor. Carpeting comes by the roll and is fastened over your floor. Wall-to-wall carpeting can even be installed directly over an unfinished subfloor, and since carpeting is often less expensive than hard flooring treatments, this a great way to save money.

The majority of today's carpets are made of nylon, which is durable, inexpensive, and can be treated with a stain protectant. Wool is still considered the ultimate carpet material due to its durability, softness, and attractiveness, but these bonuses translate into a high price tag. Save some money by choosing a wool/nylon blend instead.

The pile, or surface of a carpet, varies in construction and density. Most carpets are tufted, meaning they are manufactured by stitching loops of yarn through a backing. In a loop pile, the loops are left uncut; in cut pile, the loops are cut. Some rugs combine cut and loop pile, and some use multiple levels of loops or cut pile to create textured patterns.

Pile also varies in density. To check the density, bend the carpet into a "U" (with the pile facing outward) to see how much of the backing shows through. The less backing you see, the denser the carpet.

Ask the Experts

My friend swears by the commercial carpet she installed in her family room. Is this kind of carpet suitable for my master bedroom?

Heavy-duty commercial, or industrial, carpet is usually used in office buildings, restaurants, and hotels, which get a lot of foot traffic and need durable floor covering. Your friend is right that it can be a good choice for a family room, especially if the room is used by a lot of people and pets. Since most bedrooms don't see this kind of action, there's no reason to use more expensive commercial carpet.

I have terrible allergies. Should I get rid of the wall-to-wall carpeting in my master bedroom?

If you're like most people who suffer from allergies, one culprit is probably dust mites, which are found in every home. Dust mites love carpets as much as we do, so unless you're a carpet-cleaning fanatic, stick with hard floors. However, you can still use small, machine-washable area rugs next to your bed for some softness.

Carpet padding

Your carpet works in tandem with a carpet pad, which is installed underneath the carpet. This padding cushions your feet and also prolongs the life of your carpet, so don't skimp by purchasing an expensive carpet and a cheap pad. Always install a new pad with your new carpet, rather than reusing an older pad. Ask your carpet dealer or contractor which pad should be used with your particular carpet.

A

B

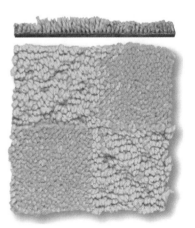

C

walls and windows

Creating a private and relaxing environment

Windows are a vital part of any room. But bedroom window placement and window dressings take some extra consideration. You want to be able to control the amount of light you let in, while maintaining your privacy

First, consider the view. Take a good long look out your existing bedroom window, or stand outside near where your new window would be installed and look around. If your view is less than noteworthy or even downright disagreeable, consider using frosted glass, which will let in the light while obscuring the view. Another solution is to double your window treatments by using blinds, shades, or a heavier window treatment against the glass, along with a sheer outer layer. To let in light during the day, draw back the heavier layer, but keep the sheer layer closed. At night, close the heavier layer for additional privacy and to block out morning rays.

If the view if fine but privacy is the issue, think about covering windows with tinted film (the kind used in car windows), which will allow you to enjoy the view while preventing anyone from seeing inside. Another option is to install **clerestory windows**: tall, narrow windows set high in the wall. They let in light but are too high to see through, meaning you won't need window treatments.

A skylight (see page 155) is also a great choice, and allows you to gaze at the sky while lying in bed. If your bedroom has an angled roofline, you can create some airiness and let in more light by adding a dormer, a small, squarish structure that projects out through the sloping roof and includes one or more windows (see page 152).

The direction the window faces, or exposure, is another important consideration. If you're not an early riser, having an eastern exposure may mean you'll be rudely awakened by the morning sun. If an east-facing window is your only choice, use lined window treatments to block the sunlight.

Quick exits

Most building codes require that rooms used for sleeping include an emergency egress window you can escape through in case the doorway is blocked by fire. An egress window must be at least 5.7 square feet, and at least 20 inches wide and 24 inches tall. It must also be no higher than 44 inches off the floor.

136

BEDROOM WALLS AND CEILINGS

The color and texture of the walls play a major role in creating the atmosphere in your bedroom. If you're ready to break out of the mold, choose a distinctive color or pattern or use architectural details (see page 112) like wainscoting.

When selecting paint or wallpaper, keep in mind that color can have a major effect on your moods, not to mention your ability to fall asleep. Red may work for a dining room or living area, but few of us would want to use this strong, vibrant color in our bedrooms.

Warm colors like red, yellow, and orange are energizing, while cool hues like blue, green, and violet—as well as soft, neutral tones like white, beige, and gray—are relaxing and soothing. Aside from the color itself, also consider its brightness and intensity, or how saturated it is. A neon blue is hardly tranquil, while a pale yellow or apricot can be quite calming. What if you're a sound sleeper who has trouble waking up? Use bright colors in a pattern or as accents on window sills and moldings to help rev you up in the morning.

And don't forget the ceiling (see pages 122–123). You can paint a mural or add decorative touches. Or consider a raised ceiling, which will give your bedroom a dramatic look. It can also make the room seem vast and open, however—not something you'd want if you like to feel cozy and snug before you fall sleep.

closet planning

Reach-ins, walk-ins, and dressing rooms

Every bedroom needs a closet. The question is what type of closet and how big? The basic closet is referred to as a wall closet or reach-in because, as the name implies, you reach in to get what you need. The minimum configuration for this type of closet is two feet deep with a rod for hanging clothes and a shelf over the rod. Many closets also have shelving on one side for folded garments. These shelves are often adjustable, allowing you to reconfigure the height for different items. Many home improvement chains sell wire or melamine closet-organization systems that will help you eke every inch of storage space out of your closet.

If you're looking to renovate your closet, you probably won't regret moving up to a walk-in closet, even if it means taking space from an adjacent room. You can walk right into a walk-in closet, which still looks like a closet inside, with clothing rods and shelves. Add built-in drawer units to store folded items.

You can even go beyond the walk-in closet to create a dressing room. These larger rooms can be quite elaborate, resembling a small personal boutique devoted to your clothing, accessories, and the art of accoutrement. Your dressing room can include built-in drawer units and shelves for knits, undergarments, and shoes, as well as clothing rods for shirts, jackets, and other hanging items. You can leave the shelves open so you can find everything easily, or put everything behind doors to create a closet-within-a-dressing-room. Complete the luxurious environment with full-length mirrors, a chair for putting on shoes, a dressing table, a window, and perhaps an ironing board.

Ask the Experts

I'd love to have a walk-in closet but don't have the space. Any solutions?

Before you write off a walk-in closet, think about your clothing storage needs. If you're like most of us, you need a reach-in closet as well as a dresser. If you opt for a walk-in closet with shelves for folded items instead, you'll most likely be able to eliminate the dresser, freeing up floor space you can incorporate into the walk-in closet.

My friend tells me I should use cedar for the walk-in closet I'm planning. Why?

Have you ever pulled a garment out of your closet and noticed mysterious holes? The culprits are most likely moths, whose larvae feed on natural fibers. Aromatic cedar naturally repels moths, as well as mildew. But be aware that your clothing will smell like cedar if you line your closet with it. As with any strong scent, some people love it, some are indifferent, and others hate it, so get a good whiff of aromatic cedar before you commit to using it.

FIRST PERSON DISASTER STORY
A room of one's own

My husband and I each used to have a separate reach-in closet. We decided to demolish them and create one large walk-in closet for both of us. Well, we both overlooked the fact that he's very neat and I'm totally disorganized. It's driving him nuts to walk into that closet and be confronted by my disarray, but it's hard enough for me to keep the house and bedroom under control, never mind the closet! Needless to say, we've had a few arguments about the state of our shared space, and both think it would have been better to stick to separate closets.

Corinne B., Sandusky, Ohio

children's bedrooms

Do you remember your childhood room? It was your own little haven where you could sleep, read, play, and daydream—and, when you got older, enjoy some precious privacy.

At the very least, children need a bedroom that provides a comfortable environment for sleeping and a closet for storing clothing. If you don't have a playroom, family room, or finished basement, your child will most likely also use the bedroom for playing, socializing, and studying, and will need ample storage space for books, papers, toys, games, and the numerous other objects children manage to collect. That's a lot of function to fit into what are often some of the smallest rooms in your house.

Add to this the fact that children grow and change so quickly. Some parents are comfortable redoing a child's room every few years. If you would prefer not to, you'll need to consider your child's needs both for now and for the future.

A charming nursery is the dream of many expectant parents. The truth is, though, babies aren't picky about room decor! Feel free to choose a decorating scheme that makes you happy; after all, you'll be spending almost as much time in the room as your baby. Try not to give in to themed murals or wallpaper unless you're okay with changing the paint or paper as soon as your baby is old enough to tell you she prefers ballerinas to teddy bears.

Babies soon become curious toddlers, so make safety a priority. Install wall and ceiling lighting fixtures instead of using lamps that can be knocked over. Since some young children will quite readily climb up on shelves or drawers, use built-in units in lieu of dressers or shelves on brackets. For more tips on safety and childproofing a baby's room, as well as your entire house, contact the Consumer Products Safety Commission (**www.cpsc.gov**) or the Juvenile Products Manufacturers Association (**www.jpma.org**).

Even when the destructive toddler phase is over, children still need rooms that can hold up to typical children's activities. After all, no child wants to live in a room that feels like a museum. Use floor coverings that can be cleaned easily and replaced inexpensively, if need be, such as a laminate or resilient flooring. Carpeting or area rugs are good choices, since children spend a lot of time sitting or playing on the floor. Look for carpets treated for stain resistance, such as DuPont Stainmaster.

Walls will also need to stand up to smudges and fingerprints. Avoid paints with a flat finish in favor of gloss or semigloss versions that can hold up to washing, or use scrubbable wallpaper, which can be vigorously cleaned.

While most children's rooms have straight, boxy walls, building in some nooks and niches will help zone the room and create little areas for different activities. They're especially helpful for defining territory when two or more children have to share a room.

Older children and teens spend even more time in their rooms than younger kids. If you don't have space for a typical desk, you can have a built-in desk or table custom-made to fit into an awkward space or corner. Will your child have a computer, TV, and/or audio equipment in the room? Include enough grounded outlets to protect the components from power surges, and extend high-speed wiring into children's rooms (see page 110).

guest bedrooms

Options for dedicated vs. dual-purpose guest rooms

The guest bedroom means different things to different people. If you have lots of out-of-town friends and family you want to accommodate, you might want a large guest room with a private full bath to create an almost bed-and-breakfast-like atmosphere.

If overnight guests are infrequent, you will probably opt for a small, minimal guest room, or one that can serve another function when guests aren't around.

Consider who your guests are and how often and how long they stay. A younger guest who only stays for a night or two will be comfortable sleeping on a sofa bed or futon. Someone staying for a longer period, as well as older people or those with back problems, might need a real mattress and box spring in order to feel their best the next morning.

If you have extra bedrooms to spare, a dedicated guest room is a no-brainer. Simply assign an extra room the role of guest room—or tear down a wall to transform two small bedrooms into one larger room. Opt for twin beds that can sleep two single adults or be pushed together to create a king-size bed for a couple.

If you don't have a room you can devote to guest use, create a dual-purpose guest room. Sofa beds or fold-out futons provide seating space one minute and a bed the next. Or try a Murphy bed, which lifts up and is stored out of sight in its own cabinet. Outfit the room with a computer desk and chair, or with shelves, so you can also use it as a home office, library, or playroom. French doors, pocket doors that slide into the wall, or a folding screen can be used to turn one room into two or to close off the home office when guests arrive.

Ask the Experts

I have several options for where to put a guest bedroom. What's the best spot?

Near your other bedrooms is a good choice. If this isn't feasible, try at least to leave a little distance from the main living areas. If you're not adding a private bath for guests, locate the guest room near a family bathroom or powder room. Another option is to create a guest room or suite over a garage or in a finished basement or attic. Guests will appreciate having a little extra privacy. Just make sure your guests are comfortable climbing stairs.

Should I include a closet in my guest room?

A closet is always appreciated, especially by guests staying a few days, but it's not an absolute necessity. Pegs on a wall or the back of a door may be all your guests need for hanging items. You can clean out a shelf or desk drawer so guests have a place for toiletries and personal items. If you have the extra space for a closet, remember you can also put it to use by storing your extra clothing or seasonal items in it.

What are the best wall and flooring treatments for a guest room?

Carpeting is a good choice since it's soft under bare feet. If you'll also be using the room for crafts or hobbies, or as a playroom, you might prefer to use a laminate or vinyl floor, which can stand up to heavier use. Remember that today's guest room may become tomorrow's nursery or laundry room, or it may disappear altogether when you expand a kitchen, bathroom, or master bedroom. So, unless you're positive it will remain a guest space for years, keep it simple.

now what do I do?

Answers to common questions

What are the best colors for bedroom carpets?

A solid color will present one unbroken surface and thus make the room seem larger. A patterned carpet can be eye-catching, but may distract from other decorative elements in the room. A white carpet is asking for trouble, since it will show every speck of dirt, while lint will be prominent on dark solids. A carpet in a dark-colored pattern is best at hiding dirt and a good choice if you are not very diligent about vacuuming and carpet cleaning.

We're redoing our five-year-old daughter's room. She wants a beautiful wallpaper that will stretch our budget. Should we pick it anyway, since it's her room and it's what she really wants?

You're on the right track by involving your child in her room renovation, but that doesn't mean you have to give her carte blanche. Children don't understand the work and money involved in renovating. They can also tire of things quickly, and you may find today's longed-for wallpaper covered with posters or artwork tomorrow. See if you can find bedding, window treatments, and accessories in the same colors or theme instead. Or paint a wall with chalkboard paint. Children can write in chalk and erase their creations, just as if they were using a real blackboard.

I want to use some of my current guest room space to expand my master bedroom, but I don't want to lose the guest room altogether. What is the minimum amount of space I need for a guest room?

All overnight guests really need is a comfortable place to sleep and enough clearance to move around the bed comfortably. A twin bed is 39 by 75 inches, a full-size bed is 54 by 75 inches, a queen is 60 by 80 inches, and a king is 78 by 80 inches. Choose your bed size, then leave about 15 inches of clearance space around at least two sides of the bed. There are other, more esoteric bed sizes, such as the California King, but keep in mind that it could be difficult to find bedding to fit them.

I have allergies. What else can I do aside from not using carpeting?

It's important to keep your bedroom as free of irritants as possible so you can get a good night's sleep. Use a hypoallergenic mattress or mattress cover. Forgo dust collectors like dust ruffles, canopies, drapes, upholstered furniture, carpets, and moldings in favor of a less fussy, more minimalist approach: bare walls, window shades, and a hard floor with perhaps a throw rug or two. If your allergies are very bad, install a central vacuuming system that will draw dust through pipes in the walls to a container located outside the house.

The new wall-to-wall carpet I installed in my master bedroom is shedding. Is there something wrong with it?

Probably not. And don't blame your dog or cat for scratching it up (although they may indeed be doing this). Some new carpets, particularly wool ones, shed for several days after installation. Just vacuum it daily and eventually it will stop shedding.

I work a night shift and have trouble sleeping in my sunny bedroom during the day. Any tips?

Try blackout curtains, which are lined with a material that is more effective at blocking sunlight than regular window coverings. You can purchase them from Web sites like **www.blackoutcurtains.com** and **www.comforthome.com**.

Now where do I go?

BOOKS

Simple Solutions: Bedrooms
by Colleen Cahill

Bedrooms
by Chris Casson Madden

The Smart Approach to Children's Rooms
by Megan Connelly

WEB SITES

The Carpet and Rug Institute
www.carpet-rug.com

DuPont Stainmaster Carpets
www.stainmaster.com

California Closets
www.calclosets.com

Chapter 8

Attics

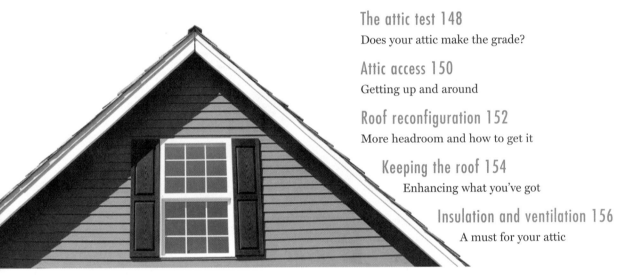

the attic test

Is your attic a candidate for renovation?

An attic presents a wonderful opportunity to create extra living space. You've already got a floor, a roof, and walls. All you have to do is add insulation and ventilation; run electrical, heat, and possibly plumbing lines; install windows and doors; and finish everything off with paint, wallpaper, and flooring. The attic's remote location makes it a perfect choice for rooms that benefit from additional privacy, such as a master bedroom suite or a home office.

But your attic will need to meet certain criteria before you can move ahead with your renovation. An attic used as living space will have to bear the extra weight of people and furniture, something it didn't have to do as an unfinished attic. Consult an architect or structural engineer to find out if your house can handle the burden; otherwise you'll have to strengthen your existing walls or foundation, and perhaps put in stronger floor joists. Factor in these costs, as well as the price of heating and cooling the extra space. And remember to check for leaks, rotting beams, and other structural problems, and include the cost of repairs into your budget.

FIRST PERSON DISASTER STORY
Fooled by the floor

When I went up to check out my attic, I saw rafters with what I thought was a floor directly underneath. But when I stepped between the rafters onto the so-called "floor," my foot crashed right through! Luckily, I was able to pull my leg back out. I wasn't hurt, aside from my wounded pride at having to explain to everyone why we now had a mysterious hole in our downstairs ceiling. Now I realize our unfinished attic floor was constructed of drywall that wasn't intended to hold much weight.

Arthur L., Ogden, Utah

FRAMING AND CEILING HEIGHT

Finishing an attic is only an option if you have a high attic, or one with enough ceiling height for you to stand up in, as opposed to a low attic, or crawl space. But not every high attic is a suitable candidate for remodeling—it depends on what kind of framing and support system your attic has.

Rafter and collar-beam system In this system, the attic walls and the ceiling are framed with 2-by-6 or 2-by-8 beams and ceiling rafters (a series of parallel beams that support the roof). These rafters run from the ridge beam—the beam that runs along the middle of the roof—down the slope of the roof to where it meets the floor or wall. You can't remove the collar beams, so as long as they are high enough, you should have no problem converting this type of attic into living space.

Truss system If instead the beams of your attic are arranged in a crisscrossed or W shape extending vertically from ceiling to floor, then your attic has a truss system. Trusses are made of plywood or synthetic material and are not as thick as rafters. Trusses all work together as a system; remove or modify even one and you'll be compromising your house's structure and may even cause your roof to collapse.

Even if your attic is the right type, you're not free and clear to proceed just yet. In order to meet most building codes, a room used for living space needs to have a ceiling height of 7.5 feet over at least 50% of the floor area. You can, however, add dormers (see pages 152–153) to help you meet this requirement.

attic access

Staircases and ladders

Most unfinished attics are simply equipped with a pull-down ladder, or even just a trapdoor. Not only will you want a staircase going up to your remodeled attic, but you are required by building codes to provide one to connect levels used as living space.

Surprisingly enough, the hurdle of figuring out where to put the staircase can sometimes make or break the decision of whether to proceed with an attic renovation. Staircases take up a lot of space, both in the attic and on the lower level. If you don't have a lot of room to spare, you may have to forfeit part of a downstairs room or lose a closet.

Even if you already have a staircase leading to your unfinished attic, it may have to go. That's because staircases leading to living spaces must comply with a multitude of building codes, from the size and distance between steps to the dimensions of landings and banisters. Complying with code will give you a safer staircase as well as one that will pass inspection with your building department.

Depending on how much space you have, your staircase can take many forms:

■ A standard staircase rises diagonally, with no additional landings.

■ A circular or spiral staircase winds up in a continuous spiral. These work well in small areas since they don't require much floor space.

■ A landing staircase has an extra landing halfway up; the top half of the staircase usually ascends in a different direction than the bottom half. If you have any difficulty climbing stairs, this landing will give you a chance to catch your breath between flights.

■ Winding stairs either curve after two or more straight steps or consist of one graceful, gradual curve.

Ask the Experts

Who should I hire to build a staircase for me?

A carpenter can build a basic staircase or one that isn't on view, such as stairs to an unfinished attic or basement. For anything more elaborate, it's best to go with a company that specializes in staircases. Specialists can advise you on which type of staircase would work best in your home, and they're knowledgeable about the many building codes that dictate stair dimensions. The stairways are usually built in a workshop and then assembled in your home.

I love the look of a spiral staircase. But if I put one in, how will I get my bed and other large items up into my new attic bedroom?

It's true that the narrow twists and turns of a spiral staircase can make it impossible to transport large objects upstairs, but there is a solution. Put in a spiral staircase, but also install a trapdoor with a pull-down ladder in another location. The ladder can be used when you need it to transport bulky items, then folded up out of sight when not in use.

roof reconfiguration

Adding dormers or raising the roof

What do you do if your attic doesn't include enough headroom, or if you just want to open it up and let in more light?

The most common solution is to add a dormer, a window set vertically so that it projects through a sloping roof. A rectangular hole is cut in your roof and the dormer is constructed to fit into the hole and work with the existing roof framework.

Gable dormers

Dormers fall into two categories: gable dormers and shed dormers. Gable dormers are typically 4 to 7 feet wide, with rafters that meet in an A-frame roof with a ridge beam, so that they resemble miniature houses with a window and peaked roof. Shed dormers have a flat, sloping roof and are larger; they can range from about 12 feet wide to the entire width of your house.

Dormers can help you meet building codes by increasing the amount of headroom and enabling you to install the required number of windows. According to most codes, eight percent of the total wall area of a room used for living space must include windows, half of which must be operable windows (windows that can be opened). Locate operable windows on opposite sides of your attic so you can take advantage of cross breezes to air out and cool the space.

If your attic will contain a bedroom, building codes require that you include an emergency exit in case of fire. This can be a door that leads to an attic deck and staircase, or an egress window that is easily accessible and large enough for a person to climb through (see page 136). You can purchase an emergency escape ladder that can be rolled up and stored under the bed or in a closet, and then attached to the window and unrolled if needed. For more fire safety tips, contact the National Fire Prevention Association (**www.nfpa.org**).

Ask the Experts

We would like to put in dormers. How do we live with having a hole in our roof for several weeks?

Make sure the contractor spells out in your contract how this potential problem will be handled. You'll want to specify that the openings are covered with plastic sheeting or some other protective covering at night or on days when it's raining and work cannot proceed. Also, try as best as you can to schedule construction for the warm, dry times of year.

My architect is trying to persuade me to add two gable dormers so the house looks better from the street. I only need—and want to pay for—one.

A good architect has an eye for how your home should function and look, and knows that a dormer will change your house's exterior appearance, as well as the inside of your attic. Gable dormers do traditionally travel in pairs, and a small gable by itself can look slightly comical, especially if your home is on the large side. You might regret adding just one after you see what it looks like. Building two dormers now, or one larger shed dormer, will be less expensive and time consuming than going back to redo the job later. Besides, you probably won't regret the extra light and headroom.

Dormers aren't enough for me. How difficult is it to raise the roof?

You'll have to completely remove your old roof, change the height of the walls, and put on a new roof. This takes more time, labor, and money than building a dormer, but you will get the ceiling height you want. A less expensive option is to raise the walls and roof over one section of your attic and leave the rest of the roof as is.

keeping the roof

Making the most of quirky angles

Your budget may not leave room for dormers, never mind a new roof. Or maybe you've always loved attic rooms and considered the odd angles and exposed chimneys to be part of their character. In any case, you'll still have to work around obstructions and parts of the attic you won't be able to stand in. So how exactly do you create a room that's as functional as it is attractive?

Most rooms need to include space for sitting, sleeping, or storage. The trick is to locate these areas against the knee walls—the three- to four-foot-high walls that start at the floor and rise vertically to intersect with the attic's sloping ceiling. Angle a bed so that the foot or side rests against a knee wall, or place chairs against one to create a sitting area. The lack of headroom also won't matter for a desk or a bathtub placed under the slope.

Built-in storage units (see pages 184–185) are another perfect companion for knee walls. Build them to fit precisely into one to make the best use of this space.

Most attics contain chimneys and plumbing stack pipes; yours could have these against an exterior wall or even in the middle of the attic. Unless you want to go to the expense of relocating these, you'll have to make do by leaving them in place, perhaps concealing them if you find them unsightly. Have an enclosure, shelves, or a bookcase built around them. If your attic will include more than one room, this is a great place to build a partition wall.

SKYLIGHTS

Skylights are windows set in a roof, rather than a wall. They're a natural for the sloping roof walls of an attic, and can offer light, and possibly ventilation, as well as views of both sky and land.

Skylights (also referred to as "sky windows") can be dome, or bubble-shaped, or flat, just like regular windows. Bubble skylights are a good choice for a flat roof, since they won't become clogged with snow, leaves, or debris.

You can choose either fixed or operable skylights. Fixed skylights cannot be opened and are the least expensive option. Operable, or vented, skylights can be propped open or opened via a hand crank or remote control. They can help cool your attic by letting rising hot air escape.

While skylights offer some lovely benefits, the fact remains that, like any window, they don't pack the insulating power of a wall, so you will have some heat loss in the winter. As with other types of windows, you'll need to check your exposure. Northern- and eastern-facing skylights will admit less light than southern and western exposures, but the latter two will also cause your attic to heat up quite a bit. Protective tints and coatings will help in the summer by reflecting sunlight, but can also let in less light in the wintertime. Another solution is to purchase shades or blinds to fit the skylight. Or place a skylight where it will be shaded by a tree that's leafy in summer (to help keep the heat out) and bare in winter (to let much-needed winter sunlight in).

insulation and ventilation

Keeping a potential hot spot cool

If you're finishing your attic, you'll need to take insulation and ventilation very seriously in order to be comfortable in your new space. Most locales have stringent codes regulating how much venting and insulation a room must have. An improperly insulated and ventilated attic room can become unbearably hot and stuffy in the warmer months. And in winter, your much-desired heat will rise to the ceiling and out through the roof, rather than keeping your house warm, so you'll essentially be sending your energy dollars out along with it.

Unused attic space often uses a passive (or static) ventilation system. This includes an intake vent at the eaves to draw in fresh air, and an exhaust vent under a gable or the ridge beam to let out warm air. Make sure your attic includes these vents, and be sure not to remove or block them during your renovation.

Roof areas that require insulation
A Attics/flat ceilings
B Attic ventilation
C Cathedral ceilings

You can take ventilation one step further by making it active, or powered. An attic exhaust fan pulls in air and expels it through a vent. You can connect your fan to a switch or use a thermostatic fan, which is hooked up to a thermostat that will automatically turn the fan on when the temperature reaches a certain level.

Ventilation works hand in hand with insulation. Unfinished attics already have insulation in the floor. If you're finishing your attic, you'll also want to put in ceiling insulation that has a vapor barrier, a layer of watertight material that prevents moisture from your home's interior from penetrating the roof, where it can condense and damage not only the insulation but your house's structure. The vapor barrier should always be placed facing your living space.

Insulation is graded by R-values. The higher the R-value, the better the insulation. Depending on where you live, your R-value should be anywhere from 30 to 40.

Ask the Experts

The floor of my unfinished attic already includes insulation. Should I just leave it in?

Probably not. Most likely the existing insulation has a vapor barrier, which is used to separate heated living space from unheated rooms or the outside. If you plan on heating your finished attic, you'll need to replace this with insulation that does not have a barrier. If there is no barrier in the existing insulation, you can leave the insulation in, or add new insulation on top of it. Insulating the floor can help keep your attic and the lower levels more comfortable, as well as provide extra soundproofing.

An engineer inspected our attic ceiling and said we'll have to replace part of our roof because of damage caused by ice dams. What is he talking about?

You're lucky to catch this problem now, before it gets even worse. Even small attic crawl spaces perform the important function of venting hot air away from the roof and thus keeping it cool. If you live in an area that has cold winters, a roof that's too warm will cause ice and snow to melt, trickle down your roof, and refreeze to form ice dams at the eaves. Water collects behind the ice dams, where it eventually seeps into and damages both your insulation and your house's structure. Proper insulation and ventilation will prevent ice dams from forming again.

Can I put in insulation and ventilation myself?

While laying in insulation and installing vents is a fairly easy do-it-yourself project, it helps to have expert advice from an HVAC specialist or contractor. The best methods for insulating and ventilating can vary, depending on the climate for your region and even your roof pitch. If you do install fiberglass insulation yourself, be sure to wear long sleeves and pants and a face mask to prevent irritation from any stray fibers. Although most newer types of insulation are encased in a sleeve that contains the fibers, it's always better to play it safe.

heating and air conditioning

Extending systems or adding zones

When it comes to heating your attic, your first step is ask your contractor or HVAC specialist if your existing furnace or boiler can handle heating the extra space. If it can, you can simply add ductwork or pipes up there and connect them to your system.

If your furnace can't handle it, you have three choices. You can buy a larger furnace. If your current unit is over 10 years old, you may save money in the long run by replacing it with a newer, more energy-efficient model. If it's less than 10 years old, replacing it is probably not an economical solution. You may be better off purchasing a small additional furnace to heat your attic space. Another option is to add electric heating units, such as baseboard heaters. Although the units themselves are inexpensive, electric heat is costly, so this isn't a good choice if you live in a very cold region.

If you extend your existing heating system, you may be able to put your attic on a separate heating zone (as long as you don't have an older or forced hot-air system). Zoning is a way to partition areas in a house so that the heat in each area is activated by its own thermostat. Since heat rises, zoning would allow you to heat your downstairs to a comfortable level without overheating the attic, saving your energy dollars.

The heating pipes or ducts, as well as electrical wiring and phone lines, can be run inside the walls or under the floor. The more walls you include in your attic, the more choices you have for where to put heating lines and electrical outlets. If your attic will be one large home office or exercise room, you'll have just the exterior walls to work with.

KEEPING COOL

Aside from ventilation, you may want to have other ways to cool your attic when the weather gets hot.

Air conditioning can be provided via a central air conditioning system or individual units installed in the walls. With central air conditioning, the cooling unit, or condenser, is located outside your house and the cooled air is pumped in through a system of ducts.

If you have central air conditioning, consult your contractor or HVAC specialist to find out if your condenser is large enough to handle your attic. If it is, you can simply run connecting ducts into the attic. If the unit isn't large enough, replacing it is so expensive that you'll probably want to go with separate, self-contained window units.

When purchasing a window air conditioner, it's important to determine the BTU you need so you can buy the right size unit. If the air conditioner is too small, it won't cycle off often enough and will waste energy. If it's too large, it will cool the room too quickly and not give it enough time to dehumidify, making the room feel cold and clammy.

To find the right BTU, multiply the length of the room by the width, then multiply the result by 35. For instance, for a 10-by-12-foot room, multiply 120 by 35 and you get 4,200 BTU. This formula is based on having no more than two people in a room with a ceiling up to eight feet high. For each added foot or additional person, add 500 BTU. If the room is very sunny, increase the BTU by 10 percent; if shady, decrease it by 10 percent.

now what do I do?

Answers to common questions

I'd like to add a bathroom when I renovate my attic. What do I need to know?

Before you jump into your attic renovation, you'll need to have an architect or structural engineer determine whether your attic floor can handle the extra weight. Tile floors and fixtures like toilets, showers, lavatories, and tubs are all very heavy. You certainly don't want a bathtub plunging through the attic floor—and the downstairs ceiling! But don't panic if your floor doesn't pass muster. Your floor can be strengthened with additional joists or other means of support.

We have a low attic, with only about four feet of headroom—certainly not enough for a new room. Is there any other way we can use the attic?

Not all of us are lucky enough to have an attic we can stand in. But you can put your low attic to good use by turning it into storage space that doesn't make you break into a sweat the minute you get there. Proper insulation and a good exhaust fan will help keep your attic comfortably cool. Add a drop-down ladder for better accessibility and an attic light that connects to a switch on the lower level, so that you can turn it on before ascending.

Attic exhaust fans are so unattractive. Can't I use a ceiling fan to ventilate my attic?

Ceiling fans make rooms feel cooler by moving air and can help reduce your air conditioning costs. However, they are not nearly as powerful as an air conditioner, nor are they a replacement for a less picturesque attic exhaust fan. Luckily, you can install an exhaust fan into the roof or at the top of a wall so that it's barely noticeable. If your attic still gets too hot for comfort, you may need to install an air conditioner.

I like the idea of having a vented skylight, but a fixed one would be cheaper. How do I decide which one to install?

Where do you plan to place the skylight? A vented skylight won't do you much good if you rarely open it, and if it's over your head on the ceiling, chances are you won't bother. On the other hand, if it's on a sloping roof wall, at eye level, you'll probably appreciate being able to open it up for air. If the skylight will be in a bathroom, a vented unit is a good idea, since it will enable you to cut down on humidity.

You should also take into consideration how many operable windows you'll be adding to your attic, then decide whether you need the skylight to provide ventilation so you can fulfill your window code requirements (see page 155).

My architect says we absolutely have to leave the collar beams on my attic ceiling. Why?

Your architect must feel your house needs the structural support. Although you can't remove those collar beams, if you have enough headroom, you can put in a flat or dropped ceiling made of drywall that will cover them. A flat ceiling that's lower than the roof offers the added advantage of giving you a place to install electrical connections and lighting fixtures, and hides unsightly electrical wiring.

Now where do I go?

BOOKS

Better Homes and Gardens: Attics: Your Guide to Planning and Remodeling

Remodeling Basements, Attics, and Garages
by Jane Cornell

Converting Garages, Attics, and Basements
by Jeff Beneke

WEB SITES

Velux Skylights
www.velux-america.com

Owens Corning
www.owenscorning.com

The Heating and Ventilation Institute
www.hvi.org

Chapter 9

Basements

basement possibilities

Popular uses for refinished basements

Think of your basement as your home's Cinderella: a dark, damp, dingy space just waiting for a little renovation magic to turn it into a clean, bright, attractive new room for a lot less money than you'd spend on an addition.

The basement's natural soundproofing capabilities make it a great playroom, recreation room, or home theater. The sturdy concrete slab floor means you don't have to worry about floor strength and can easily create a laundry room, workshop, or exercise room, or add a bathroom or kitchenette. You can even use the basement's darkness to your advantage by turning it into a home theater, darkroom, or wine cellar.

Before you get too excited about your basement's potential, you'll need to make sure it includes enough headroom. Building codes dictate that rooms used for living space, as opposed to storage, must have ceilings that are at least 7 1/2 feet high over 50 percent of the floor area.

Now consider the type of basement you have. If your house is on a sloping grade, you may have a walkout basement, with one side above ground. A standard basement is 75 percent underground. There may be some small windows at the tops of the walls. Due to limited air circulation, standard basements tend to be cooler, darker, and stuffier than walkouts, so you'll have to work harder to make this type bright, warm, and ventilated.

Now look around to see what condition your basement is in. If you find cracks that are more than 1/4-inch wide or walls that are bowing severely, consult a foundation- or basement-repair specialist before you proceed with your renovation.

BASEMENT INVADERS: RADON AND ASBESTOS

As potential-packed as your basement may be, the fact remains that two nasty substances could be lurking there—radon and asbestos. If inhaled over a period of time, either one can increase your risk of lung cancer. If either substance is found, you'll have to deal with it before your basement can undergo its makeover. In fact, even if you are not planning to renovate, its important to check for these substances, especially if you live in an older home.

Radon is a radioactive gas found within the earth. It can seep into your basement through cracks in the walls or floor. You can test for radon yourself using a radon detection test kit, available at most home improvement stores. If the test detects a high level, contact a radon technician to perform more tests. The solution can be as simple as sealing cracks, or as complex as installing a ventilation system that releases radon outside.

Asbestos is a fibrous material once commonly used in basements as a fire retardant around furnaces or as insulation around heating pipes. It may also be in a home's old floor tiles. If you suspect there is asbestos in your home, never try to remove it yourself. Contact a certified asbestos technician. Sometimes encapsulating, or sealing the asbestos between other materials, will solve the problem. If the asbestos can't be contained, it will have to be removed.

from damp to dry

Common water problems and solutions

The common image of a basement is of a damp, musty space. Unfortunately, there's some truth to that image. Water just seems to naturally find a home in basements, where it can damage your foundation, not to mention furniture, carpeting, and other items you would put in a renovated room. The best plan is to eliminate water now in order to save yourself some major headaches later.

Basement water problems fall into four categories:

Condensation When warm air reaches your basement, it hits the cool surfaces of concrete and metal pipes and condenses. Use a dehumidifier to take moisture out of the air in the room. Cover exposed pipes with foam sleeve insulation. If you have a clothes dryer, make sure it's ventilated properly.

Leaks Moisture found on a pipe or a window could be due to a leak. Find the source of the leak and have it repaired.

Seepage If you find dampness or water stains on a wall or floor, water may be finding its way in through cracks in your basement walls. You'll need to check that your land slopes at a degree that enables it to channel water away from your house, that your gutters aren't clogged, and that downspouts are directing water at least five feet away from your foundation. If they aren't, install downspout extensions: horizontal pipes that connect to the bottom of your downspouts and release water further away from your house. Make your basement walls more watertight by filling cracks and holes with hydraulic cement or caulk.

Subterranean water Your water table lies under your basement. Sometimes after heavy rainfalls, the water table rises to the point where it will flood your basement floor. A drainage system and a sump pump will be necessary here.

Sump pump

Ask the Experts

This all sounds so complicated. How can I figure out whether my basement's dampness is due to condensation or seepage?

Here's one way to check: Duct-tape aluminum foil or plastic squares on your basement floor. After a few days, inspect the squares. Droplets on top mean condensation. Moisture on the bottom means water is seeping through your foundation. If the problem is severe or not easy to pinpoint, you'll need to call in a basement or foundation specialist.

How do sump pumps work?

Part of your basement slab is removed, and a trench, or sump, is dug underneath and fitted with a drainpipe that leads to the sump pump. When water starts to fill the basement sump, the sump pump redirects the water through the drainpipe to a trench in your yard that connects to a street gutter or storm drain, thus preventing the water from reaching floor level. Want to learn more about sump pumps? Contact the Sump and Sewage Pump Manufacturers Association (**www.sspma.org**).

FIRST PERSON DISASTER STORY

Making the grade

Our basement was problem-free aside from the water we found dripping down our walls. Our contractor pointed out that our property was on a downward slope, and that water was running down the slope and hitting the side of our house. We hired a bulldozer to regrade the area. I assumed my flower garden was far enough away from the house to be safe, but I didn't count on how much space bulldozers need to work, or the fact that drivers aren't too concerned with gardens. They ended up flattening a garden that took me years to plan. I guess it was my responsibility to find out if the garden was in their way and relocate the plants if necessary.

Robin M., Redmond, Virginia

heating, cooling, and insulation

Determine what is needed and where

One benefit of subterranean rooms is that they are naturally insulated by the earth. This tends to keep basements about 55°F year-round. Nonetheless, insulating and adding a supplemental heating source will warm up your basement in the colder months.

Ask your contractor or an HVAC technician if your current furnace has the capacity to heat your basement. If it does, you can extend the system by laying in new pipes or ducts. Put your basement on a separate zone so you can warm it up without overheating the rest of your house. You can put your heating pipes in baseboard heaters installed where the wall meets the floor.

If your furnace isn't large enough to heat the basement, you can replace it with a larger one or use another heating source, such as portable units or electric baseboard heaters. A fireplace (see pages 106–107) will also warm up the basement and create ambience and a natural focal point. Gas fireplaces would be a good choice here, since they generate more heat than wood-burning ones and can be vented directly through your basement wall, while the chimney of a wood-burning fireplace needs clearance from your basement straight up to the roof.

Insulating your basement walls will help keep your basement at a comfortable temperature, as well as cut down heating and cooling costs. Insulation in the walls and floor (areas that separate your basement from the outside, rather than another living area) should include a vapor barrier, or layer of watertight material. The vapor barrier will keep moisture from penetrating and damaging your insulation and foundation.

Ask the Experts

What can I do about the large, unsightly furnace that resides in my basement?

Boilers and furnaces are not only unattractive, they can be dangerous in living areas due to their hot surfaces. You could move the unit to another location, such as an outdoor shed, but a far more economical solution would be to separate this unit from your living space by enclosing it in drywall. You can put this enclosure to good use by building in shelving for storage or display.

I live in a warm climate, and I'm not sure if my basement will stay cool enough in the summer. Should I install air conditioning?

The fact that hot air rises means air conditioning may not be necessary. Try waiting out a summer first to get an idea of how hot and humid your basement feels. If you have central air conditioning, you may be able to extend your system to the basement. If you have a window in your basement, a window unit is another option, but be aware that it will obstruct a source of your basement's precious daylight.

We're remodeling our basement to give our teens a place to hang out with their friends. The new room will include a TV and stereo system. What can we do to keep their noise from invading our upstairs?

The basement's underground location gives it natural sound-proofing, but you'll still have some sound infiltration through the ceiling. If your basement will include a noisy home theater or play-room, or a bedroom that needs some peace and quiet, you can lay fiberglass sound insulation batts between the ceiling joists to keep sound from filtering through to, and from, your upper floors.

walls, floors, and ceilings

Considerations when covering concrete

A basement's structure isn't exactly inspiring. The floor is a slab, the walls are concrete, and the ceiling is a tangle of heating and plumbing pipes and electrical lines. What can you do to improve the look and feel of things?

If you plan to turn your basement into a workshop or recreation room, you could leave the floor and walls as is, maybe just painting them a more pleasing color.

If the concrete look isn't for you, you can finish off your walls and floor. The usual finishing method involves "furring" the walls—putting in a system of boards to provide a surface for nailing—then laying insulation, covering the boards with drywall, and topping the wall off with paint, wallpaper, or paneling.

Carpeting, vinyl flooring, or ceramic tiles can be laid directly over your concrete floor. Just make sure beforehand that the slab is level and smooth because imperfections will be carried through to your finished floor.

If you don't want to deal with repairing the slab, you can install a floating floor: a network of joists laid on the concrete and covered with a layer of plywood. It gives you a level surface to work with and also helps prevent any moisture on the slab from penetrating the flooring. You can insulate between the floor joists as well.

Companies like Cosella Dörken (**www.deltams.com**) and Subflor (**www.subflor.com**) offer new flooring solutions in the form of panels or plastic membranes that go right over the concrete slab and protect against cold and dampness. They can then be topped with laminate flooring or a plywood subfloor if you want a hardwood floor or carpeting.

Quick wall solutions

An attractive, one-step solution for finishing basement walls is available from Owens Corning (**www.owenscorning.com**). This finishing system features moisture-resistant wall panels consisting of a fiberglass core to provide insulation and reduce noise, topped by a fabric cover. The panels can be installed right over the concrete walls and, unlike drywall, can be easily removed and replaced if you need to access pipes or wiring or check the wall slab.

BEAUTIFYING A BASEMENT CEILING

Unlike your unadorned floor and walls, your basement ceiling has a lot going on in the form of heating ducts, plumbing pipes, and maybe electrical wiring. You have three choices for making the ceiling more attractive:

1. Leave the ceiling as is, perhaps staining the joists to give them a uniform appearance. If any pipes or ducts protrude or are distractingly obvious, you can enclose them in a soffit, or enclosed ceiling overhang. You can also opt to remove or relocate offending pipes and wires. Be sure to consult a plumber or heating contractor to determine which elements can go and which you'd be better off leaving in place.

2. Insulate the ceiling and then cover it in drywall, which can then be painted, paneled, or papered. Again, you can remove low-hanging pipes or enclose them in a soffit.

3. Install a drop or suspended ceiling. You've no doubt seen them in schools, offices, and other institutions. A metal grid is installed, and acoustic tiles are attached to the grid. Drop ceilings offer a big advantage in that they hide ceiling elements but allow you to access a pipe or lighting connection by simply popping out a tile or two, then putting them back in when you're done.

Headroom alert!

A floating floor raises your floor. A drop ceiling lowers your ceiling. It all translates into a reduction in headroom. Before you move forward with altering floors and ceilings, check with a professional to make sure the resulting headroom would still meet building code requirements for ceiling height.

windows and lighting

Brightening a dark room

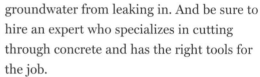

Bringing light into a room that's mostly underground is a tall order, but it can be done. This is easiest to do if you have a walkout basement with at least one aboveground wall, but you can do it even if you have a standard basement with only a thin horizontal strip of available wall.

Before you undertake this, make sure that strip is not too narrow; windows must be at least six inches above the soil to prevent groundwater from leaking in. And be sure to hire an expert who specializes in cutting through concrete and has the right tools for the job.

Another option, which will allow you to install a larger window, thus bringing in more light, and also provide an emergency exit, is to build a window well. Soil around the foundation is excavated, creating a dugout space below ground level. This can be a little longer than a window or go along the entire wall and be wide enough to place a few chairs outside. A steel, concrete, or polyethylene retaining wall is put in, and the well's floor is outfitted with a drainage system to prevent the window well from becoming a watery well after it rains or snows.

A good artificial lighting plan is also a must for your basement. Include plenty of ceiling fixtures, wall sconces, and outlets. A partition or stud wall can divide the basement into rooms and also provide a place to hide wiring. Use light colors on surfaces and furnishings, and reflective materials, like a mirrored ceiling, to help make the space seem airier.

When you're wiring for lighting, consider your other electrical needs. If you're putting in a washing machine, dryer, computer, or electronics, consult an electrician about whether you need to install separate circuit breakers.

GETTING IN AND OUT OF THE BASEMENT

If your basement includes a bedroom, building codes require that you include an exterior exit or emergency egress window that's no less than five square feet, a minimum width of 20 inches wide and 24 inches tall, and no more than 44 inches above the ground. This is large enough for you to climb through in case of fire or for emergency rescue workers or firefighters to get in.

Putting in a good-sized window or door isn't usually a problem if you have a walkout basement. If you install a door, opt for the glass variety, such as sliding or double doors, so you don't waste an opportunity to bring in more daylight. For a standard basement, a window well with stairs, tiers, or a ladder will enable you to climb out easily.

If you need to bring large items in and out of the basement, you can install bulkhead access doors: slanting, nearly horizontal double doors built outside at ground level that lead to a stairway descending down into the basement. Think of *The Wizard of Oz*, when Aunt Em, Uncle Henry, and the gang (minus Dorothy and Toto) escape to their storm cellar via bulkhead access doors.

Your basement most likely includes an interior staircase already. However, these stairs might be very steep or not include a handrail. Since building codes for staircases leading to living space differ from those going to storage areas, you may need to renovate or replace your staircase so that it meets code and is comfortable and safe to use.

bathrooms and kitchens

Installing plumbing and arranging appliances

Your basement's floor strength means that refrigerators, showers, bathtubs, and even hot tubs and saunas can find a home there without you having to worry a bit about reinforcing the floor.

If you or family members will be spending a great deal of time in the basement, consider adding a bathroom. Think about how big you want the bathroom to be—full size, half bath, or powder room. Install partition walls to separate the bathroom from living areas.

Although you probably won't want to add a full kitchen, a kitchenette with a refrigerator, sink, countertop or table, and microwave will give you a place to prepare snacks or keep your kids and their friends from invading your upstairs kitchen.

Since kitchens and bathrooms involve water, try to locate these areas next to your drain line and vent stack. If you can't find a location near enough, you'll need to cut through the slab floor and lay in pipes that connect to the main line.

Bathrooms also must be properly ventilated. If installing a window isn't an option, you'll have to install a ventilation system consisting of an exhaust fan and ducts that draw air out of the bathroom and vent it outside (see pages 90–91). This is relatively simple if your bathroom is located next to an exterior wall. If it isn't, you'll have to run vents along the walls and ceiling.

Ask the Experts

My architect says I can't include a bathroom without a sewage ejector. Why?

He is probably saying this because your main drain is located above your basement floor. Waste drain lines depend on gravity to send wastewater to the sewer, and lines must slope downward at a rate of 1/4 inch per foot. Basement fixtures can't get the job done if the drain is higher than they are. You'll need a sewage ejector, a system that pumps wastewater from fixtures up to the sewage line. One pump should be sufficient to handle all the plumbing fixtures in your basement. However, keep in mind that this is quite expensive and difficult to install. Plus, it requires battery backup and extra space, and it makes a lot of noise.

Where can I run plumbing lines for a kitchenette or bathroom?

You'll no doubt use partition walls to enclose the bathroom, and plumbing pipes can be enclosed in these walls. You can run pipes through the floor, but this will require cutting the concrete. Another option is to create a floating floor (see page 170) and run the pipes under this floor and over the slab.

I want to turn my basement into an apartment for my mother. Can I install a full kitchen?

First off, you should realize that if you want to add a second living unit to your house, you'll need to pay strict attention to a number of building codes that pertain to two-family dwellings. Next, if you want to put a kitchen in the basement, you'll need to consider how to ventilate steam and cooking fumes out of the house. It's the cooktop that's the culprit, since that's where boiling and frying take place. If you do put in a full kitchen, locate the cooktop and range hood on an exterior wall. You'll also need to have a hole drilled into the upper part of the wall to run the vent for the hood.

laundry rooms

Appliances and amenities

The laundry room tops many homeowners' wish lists as a room they most want to improve or build. While many people choose to put the laundry room near the kitchen or on an upper floor near bedrooms, basement laundry rooms have the advantage of keeping noisy appliances and piles of clothing away from the rest of the house.

Laundry rooms are changing from mere utility rooms into larger spaces that enable you to handle all your clothing-care chores in one area. Install a sink for presoaking garments or hand-washing delicates, put in cabinets for cleaning supplies, or add counter space for folding clothing. Pullout bins will provide a place for sorting laundry. And don't forget a drop-down ironing board and a clothes rod for hanging ironed garments. Don't want to lug laundry baskets

down to the basement? Check your building codes (and budget) to see if you can install a laundry chute.

Like kitchens and bathrooms, laundry rooms can also be multifunctional. If you have space, consider allocating room for a TV, desk, or exercise equipment. While waiting for a spin cycle to end, you can surf the Internet or help the children with homework. The laundry room counter may also be a great spot for potting plants or setting up a gift-wrapping or crafting station.

But no matter how the laundry room might evolve, washing machines will still have to connect to the plumbing line and dryers will still need to vent their hot, humid air outside. You can avoid some hassles by locating your laundry room right under your main plumbing line and on an exterior wall for the dryer vent. Otherwise you'll need to run plumbing pipes or vents through the floor or ceiling. For more on laundry room possibilities, check out Whirlpool's family studio (**www.family-studio.com**).

SELECTING A WASHER/DRYER

Here are some basic considerations to keep in mind when evaluating washers and dryers (see also page 70 on appliances):

Configuration You can choose between a side-by-side or stacked washer/dryer. Stacked units fit into a smaller space, but this configuration requires a front-loading washer since the dryer goes on top.

Front- vs. top-loading washers Top-loading machines use an agitator to churn clothing, while front-loaders tumble garments like a dryer does. Front-loaders are usually more expensive, but they use less energy, water, and detergent and are gentler on clothing. Some new top-loaders don't use an agitator and are less costly than typical front-loaders.

Gas vs. electric dryers If you have gas line, a gas dryer is a good choice because it is more energy efficient. It will cost a little more, but save you money in the long run.

Capacity Your typical laundry load is determined by the size of your household and how frequently you do laundry. Consider your laundry habits now and how they might change in the future.

Energy efficiency Compare the energy usage of various models by checking the Energy Guide labels (see page 71).

Special features Compare features and decide which ones you're likely to use and are therefore willing to pay for. Some new models aim to take all the guesswork out of doing laundry. In General Electric's Harmony line, the washer communicates electronically with the dryer so it can set itself for the right drying mode. Whirlpool's Duets line has a dryer with a stationary rack for items like sneakers or stuffed animals. Other dryers have automatic moisture sensors that shut the dryer off when clothing is dry.

now what do I do?

Answers to common questions

Can I use a short-term test to check for radon, or is it really better to use a long-term one?

Ideally, anyone renovating a basement—and *all* homeowners, actually—should do a long-term test in which sensitive equipment is set up for several months. Unlike a short-term test, which gives a reading based on a 48-hour period, the long-term test takes into account fluctuations in the amount of radon over time for a more accurate reading. Realistically, most of us don't want to spend the time and money for the more complex procedure unless we have to. At a minimum, everyone should perform a short-term radon test at least once. If the reading is high, call in a radon technician to perform further tests.

My basement slab floor is uneven and has so many cracks it would take me forever to seal them. Can I just install a floating floor?

Even though a floating floor doesn't require a smooth, level surface, it's a good idea to repair cracks first so that they don't allow moisture to possibly seep through and cause damage. That doesn't mean you have to repair each crack individually. You can spread a self-leveling compound or lay a new slab of fresh concrete over the old one. But because fresh concrete secretes moisture, you'll have to wait about a year before finishing it off with tile or resilient vinyl flooring. Cracks more than 1/4 inch wide could mean serious foundation problems, so consult an engineer or foundation specialist before you proceed.

Our contractor set up a sump pump system. Now he tells us we'll have to wait a year before proceeding with our basement remodeling. Why?

He wants to see if your new system solves your water problem and performs through at least one rainy season. No one likes to delay a much-desired renovation, but the hard truth about basement renovation is that if you find a problem, it can take a while to solve it and make sure the solution works. Asbestos testing and removal, long-term radon testing, waiting to see if a ventilation system is properly venting the radon, trying out a sump pump—these things take time. Take heart that even with the extra expense and the waiting game, your basement renovation could still cost you less than building an addition. Plus, you'll be solving water and hazardous-substance problems you would eventually have needed to correct anyway.

What are some guidelines for creating a home theater in my basement?

With their lack of light and natural sound insulation, basements lend themselves beautifully to home theater use. Since hard surfaces tend to distort sound, use a soft floor covering, sound-absorbing drywall or corkboard on walls, and acoustic tiles on the ceiling. If you want your basement to be a dedicated media room, limit the number of windows. Otherwise, you can add windows and cover them with sun-blocking shades for daytime movie viewing. Remember that if you'll be keeping electronics in your basement, eradicating moisture problems is even more imperative, since humidity can damage electronic components.

Now where do I go?

BOOKS

Hometime Basements How To

Better Homes and Gardens: Basements: Your Guide to Planning and Remodeling

Better Homes and Gardens: Complete Basements, Attics, and Bonus Rooms

WEB SITES

The American Association of Radon Scientists and Technologists
www.aarst.org

DeLonghi dehumidifiers
www.delonghi.com

Whirlpool
www.whirlpool.com

General Electric
www.ge.com

Maytag
www.maytag.com

Chapter 10

Storage solutions

planning for storage

If you find yourself constantly searching for places to put things or have many items that seem to have no home, a storage renovation just might be in order.

Don't feel guilty about being overwhelmed with belongings. Some homes don't include unfinished attics, basements, or garages that can be devoted to storage space. Open-plan living has eliminated hallways and walls that were once used for closets, shelves, and cabinets. We also seem to have more belongings than earlier generations and less time to organize them. It all adds up to more stuff and fewer places to stash it.

Never fear. Storage help is on the way. The solution could be as simple as putting up a few hooks and shelves. Or you might decide to add a more complex built-in unit or an entire mudroom.

Interior designers suggest planning for more storage than you think you'll need. Heed their advice. New closets and bookcases may start off with room to spare, but that extra space disappears amazingly fast!

It's also important to take a good, honest look at yourself and the other members of your household. Are you a shopaholic with an overflowing bedroom closet, a sports enthusiast with lots of equipment, or a bibliophile with piles of books and no place to put them? Are you good at paring down your stuff, or do you tend to hang on to mementos like your old term papers?

If you feel overwhelmed by your possessions and want to change your habits, there are plenty of books, as well as organizational consultants, with sound advice. Otherwise, realistically assess your style and plan on storage that will accommodate your needs.

Storage tips for pack rats

Do you have a hard time containing your clutter? Don't fight it; find a decorating style that works with it, such as a casual, lived-in Country look or the Victorian style, which features lots of collectibles and knick-knacks. Stay away from minimalistic decorating styles, such as Midcentury Modern, which favors a clean, spare, and uncluttered look.

STORAGE IN A NUTSHELL

Finding the right storage solution can be a daunting task. Start by familiarizing yourself with some basic guidelines.

First, keep like items together where you use them—this means CDs near your stereo, spices near the kitchen stove. Then consider:

Frequency of use Think of storage as consisting of active and inactive categories. Active items should be stored within easy reach; inactive objects can be kept in more out-of-the-way locations. For example, don't feel locked into storing all your cooking and baking items in the kitchen if you don't use them often. Rotating seasonal articles, like winter coats and beach paraphernalia, from inactive to active spaces may also help.

Weight Heavy items should be stored waist-high so that you can lift them comfortably without having to bend down, reach over your head, or stand on a ladder or stepstool.

Open vs. closed Open storage—think hooks on the wall, a display cabinet, or shelves—allows attractive items to be seen. Closed storage means cabinets, cupboards, and closets. You'll probably want to use both types in your home.

built-in solutions

Ways to maximize storage space

One way to solve a storage problem and keep items in use where you need them is to have a unit built to precisely fit a particular space and purpose. Alcoves, niches, and knee walls (see page 194) can be outfitted with built-ins that make use of space that would otherwise go to waste. If you can imagine it, the odds are that someone can build it for you.

The great thing about built-ins is that they're custom made to fit a space exactly. A wall is an obvious place to install built-in units or shelves, but what if your home is open plan and lacks walls? A partition wall can provide storage, as well as divide up a large space in a great room or large master bedroom, thereby separating eating or sleeping areas from those designated for working or socializing.

Window seats or banquettes are popular additions to kitchens, living rooms, dining rooms, and bedrooms, and can provide extra storage space under the seat. The storage areas are accessed either by lifting the seat or opening drawers or hinged doors beneath it.

Another solution: Instead of a bed that already has a headboard, buy a simple frame and have a headboard built that has a shelf, plus night-table surface and drawers on either side. You can even include electrical outlets and lighting connections so you can install wall sconces for nighttime reading.

BUILT-IN VS. FREESTANDING

Considering a storage unit? Built-ins and freestanding pieces both have their pros and cons.

Built-ins

Pro Since built-in units can be designed to fit an area exactly, they can make efficient use of every inch of space. You may find that one built-in can do the work of two or more freestanding pieces. You can opt for a plain, unadorned unit that will meld with the wall, or one that includes moldings and cornices that make it a decorative part of the room.

Con The downside is that you'll need to either get out your hammer or hire someone to build the unit for you. As with any custom-made piece, you usually pay more than you would for a ready-made freestanding unit.

Freestanding

Pro Freestanding storage can be a bookcase, dresser, desk with drawers, or armoire. You have plenty of options in terms of style. And while built-ins are usually made of wood, freestanding pieces can be made of metal, glass, plastic, or other materials. They can also be moved easily from room to room or replaced if you get tired of them.

Con Freestanding pieces are not usually as space efficient as built-ins.

Shaker chic

"A place for everything and everything in its place" was a motto of the Shakers, a religious community known for its simple yet beautifully made furniture. Shaker rooms had lots of floor-to-ceiling built-ins (one reason was that they saved time spent cleaning underneath and on top of cabinets) and wall pegs for hanging kitchen chairs when not in use.

closet configurations

Planning and designing extra closets

There's nothing like a closet for fitting in lots of storage. In addition to bedroom closets (see pages 138–139), you'll also appreciate having a hall closet for coats and boots or cleaning supplies, a linen closet for towels and bedding, and possibly a pantry, which is a deep-shelved closet housing foodstuffs and kitchen items.

A hall closet is a bit of a misnomer, since many homes don't have enough of a hallway to put a closet in. Luckily, this closet can fit anywhere you can afford to carve some extra space. If you have a staircase, transform the area underneath into a closet for outerwear or for cleaning equipment like mops, brooms, and vacuum cleaners.

Curious about pantries? They were once a common part of every kitchen. And guess what? They're back! Now that more and more people are buying items in bulk at warehouse clubs, the pantry has become the preferred place for storing those massive containers of peanut butter, ketchup, and dog food.

A reach-in pantry cabinet has one or two doors with shelves inside. A walk-in pantry is a small room or closet with open shelving. Pantries can be located in or near the kitchen or in a chilly area like a garage or basement. Some homeowners have even brought back the butler's pantry, a small area nestled between the kitchen and dining room that's used to store supplies like tableware and linens, and can include a sink for cleaning up or a dishwasher.

Ask the Experts

I'd like to add a closet under the stairs, but what do I do with the awkward space below the lowest stairs?

Good question. Though one side of your closet will be 8 to 12 feet high, that height will diminish the closer you get to those bottom stairs. Consider keeping the closet itself narrow and tall to store items such as coats, mops, or brooms, and using the shorter space for smaller objects. Build in drawers here, or install separate doors to get to this space more easily.

I have no room in my bathroom for a linen closet. My interior designer suggests I store towels on open shelves instead. Should I take her advice?

Colorful folded or rolled bathroom towels on a shelf are a trend in today's chic bathrooms. Although they do make a design statement, towels that sit on an open shelf for more than a day or two in a bathroom that gets daily use can soak up moisture and get mildewy. Unless you or your housekeeper is willing to air out unused towels, it's best to outfit your bath with racks for hanging towels that get used and replaced, and use a linen closet for longer-term storage.

I have little space in my bathroom for storage units. How can I store bathing supplies and towels efficiently?

In addition to a built-in soap holder, install narrow shelves near the tub or in the shower for shampoo, razors, loofahs, and the like. Home-improvement and discount stores abound with clever shower caddies and shelving systems that hang on the showerhead or squeeze into corners. And don't fret if you don't have a linen closet—your bathroom probably has at least a towel rack, and you can turn a nearby hallway closet into a linen closet for storing extra towels, as well as bed and/or table linens.

mudrooms

Packing storage and organization into a small area

Mudrooms have a sort of country-bumpkin image as a room only needed by people who frequently slog through mud or snow. But grime knows no boundaries. Plenty of homeowners have eliminated mudrooms, only to later regret their decision after having to sweep up dirt or mop up puddles in the kitchen or foyer. A mudroom can work just as hard in summer or in a sunny clime by providing a place for sandy beach towels and flip-flops or sporting equipment.

In fact, these seemingly mundane rooms have become hotbeds of design ideas. Some include laundry facilities, storage for gardening tools or pet items, counter space, or a handheld showerhead and drain for rinsing off boots (technically termed a boot-wash).

Your mudroom certainly doesn't have to be that elaborate. Typical mudrooms are about 40 square feet—big enough for two people to take off coats or pull off boots at once.

If your winters necessitate bulky coats, make closets at least two feet, two inches deep, or go for a closet that's roughly four feet deep so you can hang an extra rod behind the first one. Set rods at six feet high if you plan on storing boots underneath the coats. Also include a rack for outerwear; hooks for hats, scarves, and wet coats; shelves or drawers for gloves or out-of-season items; and cubbyholes (at least two feet deep) for boots.

Because the mudroom is an area that sees a lot of mess, make sure surfaces like walls and floors can withstand dirt, water, and plenty of cleaning. Brick is a popular flooring choice, along with ceramic tile, slate, laminate, or vinyl flooring. Choose oil paint or gloss or semigloss latex paint for walls. If you must use wallpaper, go for the scrubbable type.

MUDROOM EXTRAS

Mudrooms are a great place to organize items you need to have handy before you leave or enter the house. Include hooks for keys and a shelf for outgoing mail.

A mirror is a nice touch so you can give yourself the once-over before heading out.

A window and a ceiling light will brighten the room at night and on overcast days.

A bench will offer a spot for putting on and pulling off footwear.

If winters are particularly cold, install a door to separate the mudroom from the rest of the house. By doing this, you create an air lock: a space that keeps drafts from flowing through the house whenever someone enters.

If your mudroom is enclosed and you want to warm it up on frigid days, install radiant heat (see page 90) under the floor. Other options include an electric baseboard heater that you can switch on when you need it.

hobby and work areas

Organizing garages, libraries, home offices and hobby rooms

Chances are there are certain areas of your house you'll want to devote to work, reading, repairs, or a hobby, and that those rooms will have plenty of storage requirements.

Garage The garage has become much more than a place to park your car. Many also store home and auto supplies. Some have degenerated into catchall spaces so overrun with items that there's no longer room for a car! If this is your situation, a little organization can help.

A series of wall and base cabinets can house tools, paint, motor oil, and other items. Include a pegboard and hooks for hand tools, along with a worktable for your projects. If you store your sporting goods in the garage, buy wall or ceiling racks designed for specific types of equipment, such as skis, bicycles, bats, rackets, and balls of various sizes.

Don't forget overhead garage space. Install a ceiling rack above the car for items that aren't used too often. Most garages have a low attic space under the roof. A trapdoor and pullout ladder will enable you to make use of this space.

Home office While a simple desk and chair are enough for some people, others have moved up to a more complex home office that includes a photocopier, fax machine, computer, and peripherals (items that hook up to the computer, such as printers or scanners). You can buy or have someone design a desk and shelving unit with a pullout keyboard tray and a shelf for your computer, as well as shelves and drawers for books and paperwork.

Computers, fax machines, printers, and scanners need to be near grounded outlets, so make sure shelves have holes to run the electrical cords through. You can buy a desk or built-in that sits up against one wall, or claim an additional wall or two with an L- or U-shaped desk-and-shelf unit that will provide even more work-surface and storage space.

A dedicated home office is great, but if you can't spare a room for this function, your office can be fit into a dining room, guest room, master bedroom, kitchen, or even under a staircase.

Library Whether your library is an entire room of shelves or just one large bookcase in your living room, make it easier by keeping some book-storage basics in mind. Books vary in size, so stagger the height and depth of your shelves, from 16 inches high and 12 inches deep for large hardcovers to 8 inches high and 6 to 8 inches deep for paperbacks. Adjustable shelving will let you change the configuration as your collection evolves.

Worried about high shelves being out of reach? Try a library ladder. This ladder fastens to a rolling track on an upper shelf and can be wheeled under whatever book you'd like.

Hobby areas If you like to garden, a corner of the garage or an outdoor spot can be outfitted as a gardening area, with a worktable for potting plants and a shed or outdoor closet for storing tools. A basement or ground-floor laundry room (see pages 176–177) is another good spot for a gardening or hobby space. Dirty gloves and clothing can go right into the washing machine or laundry hamper.

home entertainment storage

Housing and organizing electronics

Way back when, home entertainment was limited to a TV that sat on a stand. Today, we have the TV, the VCR, a DVD player, a cable box, a receiver, audio components, and the need for a place to put all this equipment.

Your television should be located prominently, where it can be clearly seen by all viewers in the room. The trouble is that many of us have a love/hate relationship with the TV—we love watching it but hate the way it looks turned off, when it resembles a sort of black hole in the living room, family room, or bedroom.

If this echoes your sentiments, you can house your TV and all its accompanying components in a built-in unit or entertainment armoire with doors that hide the TV when you're not watching it. If you want to get more elaborate, opt for a cabinet with a mechanism that will raise your TV out of the bottom storage at the touch of a button. A swivel stand will enable you to angle your set to suit the positions of viewers.

There's definitely more than meets the eye when it comes to storing electronics. These components generate heat and need proper ventilation so they won't burn out. Make sure you follow the manufacturer's specifications carefully. You'll need to leave at least one inch between a storage unit and a component's sides, and six inches in the back of each shelf of the unit so that the heat can rise. And don't forget the wires. Cutouts in the bottom of the shelves or in the back of a freestanding armoire will give wires access to an outlet.

Ask the Experts

I would like to put my flat-screen plasma TV over my fireplace. Will this damage the TV?

The area over the fireplace has traditionally been reserved for paintings, but many owners like to showcase their flat-screen TVs here and hide the wiring behind the wall. It's generally safe to display your TV here, but check the manufacturer's directions first for guidelines. Then, try this simple test before you proceed. Tape a thermometer over the fireplace to the area you're planning to install the TV, build a roaring fire, and wait to see if the temperature goes above 90°F. If it does, you can still mount the TV there, but don't watch it when you have a fire burning.

FIRST PERSON DISASTER STORY
Tight squeeze

I had a carpenter measure my TV and other components and build a special unit for them. I later replaced my TV with a slightly larger model and simply put it in the same unit. When the TV died two years later, I called the manufacturer to complain. The representative asked me the dimensions of both the TV and the shelf it was stored on. Although the new TV still fit on the shelf, I'd neglected to include adequate space for ventilation, so the TV had overheated and finally burnt out. If I'd thought ahead, I could have told the carpenter to leave extra space in case I upgraded.

Tamika P., Washington, D.C.

look for unused space

Use shelves, racks, and hooks to claim areas for storage

It's time to play storage detective and search your home for dead space you can endow with a useful new function.

If you have a staircase, you may be able to fit shelves on a staircase wall or landing. Make sure that both stairs and landing are wide enough to handle the storage and still meet your local building code requirements. Or fit a built-in storage unit under the stairs.

Attics and upper floors frequently feature knee walls: low, straight walls that connect to a sloping wall. Utilize this often-wasted space by installing built-ins or freestanding units (see pages 184–185).

Other candidates for storage space are much smaller and easily overlooked. The space over a door frequently goes to waste. Put it to work with a shelf for display or for storing infrequently used items, such as baking tins or a punch bowl. Install hooks on the doors themselves or on the wall space behind them.

You can also add shelves above or below a window. And don't forget window ledges. A wide ledge will give you space for small items.

HIDDEN STORAGE: ROOM BY ROOM

Kitchen Line the insides of cabinet doors with hooks. If you have an island or peninsula, include shelving or space for an appliance underneath the countertop. Use the space between the tops of wall cabinets and ceiling for display, or continue cabinets to the ceiling for extra storage inside. Get your ceiling into the act by putting a hanging rack for pots and pans over a counter.

Bedroom Have a headboard built into the wall that includes shelves and drawers. Opt for a captain's bed that includes built-in drawers underneath. A loft bed, which is like a bunk bed with no bottom bunk, will free up floor space underneath for a desk or dresser. Clothing closets can be inexpensively outfitted with wire or melamine shelves and baskets.

Living room Put a mantelpiece over your fireplace that you can use for display. Go for coffee tables and end tables with shelves or drawers underneath. A storage ottoman is one of the most versatile pieces around. You can prop your feet on it, or use it as a table or an extra seat. Then simply lift off the top to store stray items.

Dining room Hang plate racks on the wall. A built-in unit can take the place of a freestanding hutch. Plus, it offers both open and closed storage. Buy a dining table with drawers for flatware under the tabletop.

Bathroom Hang shelves on the wall behind the toilet. Built-in shelves or wire shower caddies can hold soaps and shampoos in the shower. Install cup and toothbrush holders in the wall to free up counter space.

now what do I do?
Answers to common questions

Who can I hire to help me design a new closet or garage organization system?

You can organize your closet or garage using inexpensive organization systems you pick up at a home improvement chain, but these products can't provide the expertise of a professional. If that's what you need, find an interior designer who specializes in home storage and organization, or try a company like California Closets (**www.calclosets.com**), ClosetMaid (**www.closetmaid.com**), or GarageTek (**www.garagetek.com**), many of which provide free consultations. A specialist will analyze your storage needs and, if you decide to proceed, design a system for you and oversee the installation. A carpenter can also design and build a new closet for you.

I renovated my home to include an elegant foyer. With the kids, the dogs, and all the rain and snow we get around here, I now really regret not creating a mudroom instead. What should I do?

Most mudrooms aren't located at the front entrance anyway. If you have a back or side door, create a mudroom there. Although mudrooms are typically at least 40 square feet, even a smaller vestibule can provide a place for people to escape wind and rain, wipe their feet, remove a wet coat, and leave umbrellas—and perhaps dry off a wet dog. If your basement laundry room has an outdoor entrance, put your mudroom there, so dirty and wet clothes can go directly into the washing machine or dryer.

I would really like to add built-ins, but don't want to bother finding a qualified carpenter. What can I do?

Are you using cabinets in your kitchen or bathroom already? Stock and semicustom cabinets are making inroads into other rooms of the house. You can devote a wall to a row of cabinets in a home office or family room to store books, paperwork, or entertainment equipment. Many cabinet companies even manufacture units specifically for other rooms and storage needs.

I see a lot of metal cabinets for garage storage. What is the purpose? Won't they rust?

Metal cabinets make sense in a garage because it's where many of us store flammable substances like paint thinners, oil, alcohol, and gas for yard equipment. Even though these products are often sold in metal containers, the cabinets provide some extra protection. You shouldn't have a rust problem if you mount the cabinets on a wall so they're off the cement floor, which can get damp. If you have small children in the household, you should always store these substances in a cabinet that can be locked.

How can I decide between open and closed storage units?

A wall filled with closed cabinets can feel claustrophobic, while open shelves give an airier look. On the other hand, items in open storage are on display and need to be kept organized, as well as dusted. A compromise is to use cabinets or cupboard doors with mirrored or frosted glass, which gives you the open feeling without revealing too much. And there's certainly no reason you cannot combine closed cabinets and open shelves in the same unit.

Where should I store all my DVDs, CDs, and videocassettes?

You can add a separate shelving unit or include drawers and shelves in the same built-in you use for your electronics. Unlike other items you may need to store that vary greatly in size, each type of electronic media has specific dimensions, so you can create one drawer or shelf for DVDs and CDs, another for bulkier videocassettes, and so on.

Now where do I go?

BOOKS

Taunton's Home Storage Idea Book
by Joanne Kellar Bouknight

Organized Living: Clutter Clearing Strategies and Creative Storage Solutions
by Dawna Walter and Helen Chislett

The Storage Book
by Cynthia Inions

WEB SITES

ClosetMaid
www.closetmaid.com

Kraftmaid Cabinets
www.kraftmaid.com

GarageTek
www.garagetek.com

California Closets
www.calclosets.com

glossary

Ambient light   A source of general lighting for a room, often supplied by a ceiling fixture.

Asbestos   A fibrous material once used for insulation, now linked to causing cancer. Asbestos found in your home should be either encapsulated or removed.

Backsplash   A wall that runs from behind your sink to the bottom of the wall cabinets and protects the wall from splashing water.

Banquette   An upholstered, built-in bench, often used as a window seat.

Bearing wall or load-bearing wall   A wall that provides support to a house and can't be removed without compromising a house's structure. A nonbearing or stud wall separates rooms but provides no support.

Blueprints   The architectural plans of a building, so called because they are done in blue ink or pencil on a white background, or white on a blue background.

Building codes   Local regulations that mandate construction methods and materials.

Building inspector   A professional hired by a municipality to inspect work completed on a renovation to determine if it meets the requirements of local building codes.

Building permit   A legal document issued by your town that gives you permission to undertake a renovation.

Built-in storage unit   Shelving, bookcases, or cabinets designed to fit a specific space in a house and then fastened with screws to the studs in a wall.

Bump-out   A small addition to a room, which extends out approximately four to six feet and can be built without laying a new foundation or reconfiguring the roof.

Change order   A written request submitted by the house owner to use different methods or materials or to modify the renovation from what was specified in the original contract.

Clerestory windows   Windows set in the upper part of a wall that let in light but are too high to see through.

Contractor   A person who oversees a renovation, including coordinating the project, scheduling the inspections, and overseeing the work of subcontractors.

Crawl space   An area of a house that has insufficient ceiling height for standing. A basement or attic might consist of a crawl space.

Dado   The lower part of an interior wall, usually set off from the upper wall by a chair rail, paint, paneling, wallpaper, or other wall treatment different from the upper part.

Decorative painting   Using paint to create different patterns, textures, or a faux finish that replicates the look of another material, such as plaster, leather, fabric, or marble.

Design/build   A method in which designer and contractor either work for the same firm or work together as a team to handle both the design and construction of a renovation.

Dimmer   Lighting switch that enables you to brighten and dim a light.

Dormer   A roofed structure, almost always with windows, that projects out through a sloping roof to create more headroom or let in light.

Drywall   Also referred to as plasterboard, gypsum board, wallboard, or the brand name Sheetrock®, this consists of a gypsum core bonded between two layers of fiberboard. Drywall is fastened over wall studs and ceiling joists, then spackle is used to cover nail or screw heads and fill the joins between the drywall sheets to create a uniform surface that can be painted, paneled, or wallpapered.

Exposure   The direction a window faces (north, south, east or west), which determines the amount of light and heat a room gets and affects the appearance of colors in the room.

Fenestration   Arrangement and design of a building's windows and doors.

Foundation   A concrete base that supports a house, consisting of either the walls and floor of the basement or a ground-level concrete slab.

Fixed window   A window that doesn't open or close. Examples include bow, bay, and picture windows.

Fixture   An item that, once installed in a house, is considered a permanent part of it. Fixtures include sinks, toilets, tubs, refrigerators, and other appliances.

Framed cabinets   A style of cabinet in which the box frame around the door is exposed. Framed cabinets are considered a more traditional look; they may also have ornamentation.

Frameless cabinets   Cabinets that have doors that cover the box frame. They are usually free of ornamentation, creating a more contemporary look.

Gooseneck faucet   A tall, arched faucet that provides clearance for large pots. Also called a bar faucet.

Half bath   A bathroom that contains a toilet and lavatory but no bathing fixtures. Also called a powder room.

HEPA (High-efficiency particulate air) filter   A highly effective filter that removes dust and particles from the air. They can be used in air purifiers or vacuum cleaners.

HVAC   A term that stands for heating, ventilation and air conditioning.

Joist   One of a series of wood or metal beams that frame a house's floors and ceilings. (*See also* stud.)

Gingerbread   Wood trim cut or carved into ornate patterns and used on rooflines, windows, or doorways; this is a trademark feature of Victorian or Queen Anne–style houses.

Ground fault circuit interrupter (GFCI)   A device required by most building codes to be used for electrical outlets near water, such as in the kitchen, bathroom, or outdoors. These cut the power if there's a surge or if moisture is detected, saving you from electric shock.

Inglenook   Fireplace area that's slightly separated from the rest of the room.

Interior designer   A professional trained to design the interiors of rooms and choose materials and furniture.

Kitchen island   A freestanding storage or prep unit used in the kitchen. It may include counter space, a snack bar, a sink, or a cooktop, and may have appliances and storage underneath.

Laminate flooring   Durable, easy to clean, and affordable type of flooring consisting of a decorative print layer fused or glued to an inner core. The decorative layer can closely resemble wood, stone, or other surfaces.

Lavatory   Another word for bathroom sink.

Library ladder   A ladder on wheels that fastens to a rolling track on an upper shelf and is used for reaching items stored overhead.

Lien waiver   A document signed by each supplier or subcontractor who has done work, stating that they have been paid and will not file a lien (a claim against a property).

Moldings   Wood or faux-wood strips, sometimes highly decorative, used as decoration on a wall. Cornices, baseboards, casing, chair rails, and picture rails are various types of moldings.

Mudroom   An area or room adjacent to a exterior door that provides a place to remove and store dirty or wet outerwear.

Operable window   A window that can be opened and closed. Examples include awning, casement, sliding, and double-hung windows.

Pantry   A place for storing nonperishable foods. It can be anything from a small room or a closet to a cabinet or a pullout wire-shelving unit installed in a bank of cabinets.

Peninsula   A three-sided kitchen storage or prep unit, in which the fourth side is attached to the wall.

Radiant floor heat   A method of heating in which hot-water pipes or electric coils are installed underneath a floor's surface.

Radon   A naturally occurring radioactive gas produced underground that can penetrate basements through cracks in the foundation walls.

Rafter   A wooden beam that supports a roof and runs from the center ridge beam down the slope of the roof to the top of the walls.

Rafter and collar-beam system   A structural system for an attic in which the walls and ceiling are framed with 2-by-6 or 2-by-8 beams and ceiling rafters, which run down from the center ridge beam.

Rainbar   A showerhead shaped like a long metal bar that contains numerous openings which emit a gentle spray and mimic the effect of rainfall.

Resilient flooring   Flooring that has some elasticity or cushioning, making it easy on the feet. Resilient flooring includes vinyl, linoleum, cork, and rubber.

Ridge beam   The wooden beam that runs down the center of the inside of a roof.

R-factor or R-value   A measure of insulating capability, used in reference to insulation material or windows. The higher the R-value, the better the insulation.

Setback   A local ordinance that specifies the minimum distance that houses must be located away from the street and property lines.

Shower room   A room for showering that consists of a floor, the surrounds, a drain, and one or more showerheads. Because there are no other fixtures, a partition isn't necessary.

Soaking tub   A bathtub that is shorter and deeper than a regular tub and takes up less floor space. You sit in this, rather than lie down.

Solid surfacing material (such as DuPont Corian)   Manufactured from acrylic plastic and synthetic granules, this material often resembles granite. Solid-surfacing material is durable, nonporous, and can be repaired. It's often used for countertops, sinks, and surrounds.

Spackle A plasterlike substance used to cover nail or screw heads or to fill the joins between drywall sheets.

Stud One of a series of thin wood or metal beams that frame a house's walls, running vertically from floor to ceiling. (*See also* joist.)

Subcontractors Carpenters, plumbers, electricians, and other tradespeople hired by a contractor.

Subfloor The underlying surface upon which a finished floor is laid. It can consist of joists topped with a material such as plywood, or, if it's in a basement or first floor, a concrete slab.

Sump pump A device set into a pit dug beneath the basement floor to pump out water that would otherwise flood the basement.

Toe kick The area underneath a kitchen or bathroom base cabinet. Also called a toe space or kick space.

Truss system A structural system for an attic in which beams are arranged in a rigid, crisscrossed or W shape that extends vertically from ceiling to floor.

Universal design A method of designing residences so that they are accessible to as many people as possible, including those with disabilities.

U-value or U-factor The measure of heat loss through a window. The lower the U-value, the less heat is lost.

Vanity A cabinet or dressing table that usually contains drawers. A bathroom vanity can also include a sink mounted into the top.

Variance An exception from zoning regulations granted by your local building department.

Vessel sink A bathroom lavatory that is mounted over the counter and resembles a freestanding basin.

Vapor barrier A layer of watertight material applied to one side of the insulation to prevent moisture from penetrating your home's interior and your house's structure.

Wainscoting A wall covering—often some kind of paneling—used on the lower third of a wall.

Wet wall A bathroom or kitchen wall that contains plumbing lines.

Window seat A seating area located in the space created by a bay or bow window.

Wireless fidelity (wi-fi) A term used to describe products and networks that send and receive data wirelessly.

Work triangle The main working area in a kitchen, which consists of three points: the sink, refrigerator, and main cooking area; so called because connecting each point would form a triangle.

Zoning regulations Local land use rules that determine what structural changes you can make, including how high buildings can be and how much of your lot they can cover.

index

W

Z

about the author

Ela Schwartz is a freelance writer and journalist who has covered home remodeling, decor, and furnishings, as well as business, technology and other topics, for consumer and trade publications and Web sites. Her work has frequently appeared in the *New York Daily News* and *HFN: Home Furnishings News*. She has also handled public relations for nonprofit housing organizations in New York City. As the owner of a house that has been renovated several times and underwent additional work during the writing of this book, she is no stranger to construction dust, termite damage, and other renovation surprises.

Barbara J. Morgan Publisher

Barnes & Noble Basics
Barb Chintz Editorial Director
Leonard Vigliarolo Design Director

Barnes & Noble Basics™ *Home Renovation*
Wynn Madrigal Senior Editor
Monique Boniol Photo Researcher
Leslie Stem Design Assistant
Emily Seese Editorial Assistant
Della R. Mancuso Production Manager

Barnes & Noble Books would like to thank the following consultants for their help in preparing this book: **Mike McClintock**, author of 10 home renovation and construction books and writer of the syndicated column and radio show, "Home Sense," in Rhinebeck, NY; **Clive Ebsen**, owner of Rainier Construction and Remodeling (**www.rainierconstruction.com**) in Tacoma, WA, and the Region VI Vice President of the National Association of the Remodeling Industry.